A Rainbow Book

Where To Find
Venture Capital
A Resource Guide

Philip C. Paul, President

RAINBOW BOOKS, INC.

Library of Congress Cataloging-in-Publication Information

Paul, Philip C., 1953–
Where to find venture capital : a resource guide / Philip C. Paul.
p. cm.
ISBN 1-56825-028-2 : $19.95
1. Venture capital — United States — Directories. 2. Small business investment companies — United States — Directories. I. Title.
HG4963.P38 1995
658.15'224–dc20 95-815
CIP

Where To Find Venture Capital
A Resource Guide
Hutton Financial Services Corporation, Inc.

Published by Rainbow Books, Inc.
P.O. Box 430
Highland City, FL 33846-0430 USA
Editorial Offices Telephone (813) 648-4420
Orders: Telephone (800) 356-9315, Fax (800) 242-0036
Cover Design: Betsy Lampé
Interior Design: Virginia Condello

DISCLAIMER: This book or reference guide is designed to help you in improving your business plan, sales and raising capital. The author, Hutton Financial Services Corp. Inc. and publisher assumes no responsibility whatsoever for the uses made of this material or for the decisions based on its use, and makes no warranties, either expressed or implied regarding the contents or results of the use or contents of the book.

Neither the fore-mentioned parties nor anyone else who has been involved in the creation, production, or delivery of this book or reference guide shall be liable for any direct, incidental, or consequential damages, such as, but not limited to, loss of anticipated profits or benefits resulting from the use or from any breach of any warranty of direct, incidental or consequential damages.

Manufactured in the United States of America. Printed on acid-free paper.

Dedication

This book is dedicated to my family and close friends.
Thank you for your inspiration over the years.

Contents

Introduction

Welcome to the banking world of the '90s — an era of developmental technology entering the marketplace as never before. Competition in finding investment capital has never been as keen as in today's banking world. With competition and new technological advancements, the banking world has almost eliminated the existence of capital for start-up companies. It has also had the same adverse effect on established companies. If established companies do not have the capital needed to grow and expand, they could go out of business. Because of the complex day-to-day changes in the banking and investment environment, every business owner must make plans for future growth.

Certain questions must be answered by every current or potential business owner. One of those questions is: *Where do you get the capital you need to start a new company?*

You could go to a bank, but they only lend money to people who don't need it. You could get a loan from your family, but you know what will happen if you fail, and please believe me, the less money you borrow from your family, the better off you will be.

If you have an established company: *Where do you get the money to purchase new equipment?*

Say you have an established ten-year-old company and you just developed the greatest product in the world. But without the necessary collateral, today's banks will not lend you the capital you need to proceed with your new product line.

What happens if your company obtains large orders? *Where are you going to get the additional credit or capital needed to fill the orders?*

You could, again, try to go to a bank, but don't forget, they are not in a lending frame of mind.

This book and reference guide introduces you to the world of venture capitalists. The names, addresses, phone numbers and the areas of lending speciality of over 200 venture capitalists' offices throughout the United States are printed here. Included are listings of all 50 states' phone numbers where you can obtain information concerning programs and benefits for new and growing companies. You will find listings of government agencies and private associations that may have helpful information from employee training programs to exporting information.

Just a side note

There is one point that I must make at the beginning. The main reason for this book is to give you the names, addresses and phone numbers of venture capitalists throughout the United States. I will attempt to explain the necessary information needed to approach venture capitalists. Yet, I cannot go into complete detail or explain every step in the creation of a business plan, since different businesses will have their own set of circumstances. Each company — with its own procedures, administration, and capital requirements — requires its own tailored business plan.

Good luck with all your ventures.

The entrepreneur

The life of an entrepreneur is a very exiting and wonderful experience. Entrepreneurs have exceptional judgment, instincts, aggressiveness and resourcefulness, which contribute to their successes and fortunes. An entrepreneur must have skills and intelligence necessary to find the potential problems in their company's operation — before they become major obstacles down the road.

Anyone starting a company in today's world must know where their expertise lies and their skills end. The true entrepreneur finds the professionals who have the skills needed when necessary. True entrepreneurs can find themselves in awkward positions in everyday business life, but always find a way out. It may be unorthodox, but we do find solutions.

I have brought this matter to your attention for one reason. If you need the expertise of professionals in other areas, where you lack information or experience, don't worry. This is okay. Do not think that you must have all of the answers from the start. But you will need all the answers when you start your negotiations for your venture capital. If you need the help of a professional in marketing, top management, product design, or any other facet of your company, then find it. This could be the best move you'll ever make.

Why not go to the bank?

Today, banks are not in a lending frame of mind. It may be hard to realize, but the saying is true, "Banks only lend money to the people who don't need it." Many of the local hometown banks of the past would have made riskier loans. These days, most of the smaller, friendlier banks have been bought up by big national concerns. These new and supposedly better national banks have taken the handshake and tossed it out the window. In the '70s and part of the '80s your background, credit rating, honesty, and enthusiasm were enough for the bank to loan you the capital needed. Back then, if the banker knew you and your family, the bank would go out of its way to help you.

In the '90s, a need for loans for company expansion or start-up costs has been created due to past banking problems and current banking regulations. A huge lending gap has been created in the American way of doing business. As a result, many venture capitalist firms have been born.

Venture capitalists are now lending a larger portion of business loans and investments than ever before. They are beginning to take the place of the older, smaller banks of years ago.

Going to a venture capitalist and their firm can be as interesting as you want to make it. They are in a position to make the different and unconventional business deals of today. If you went to a national bank with anything other than a normal secured loan, they wouldn't know what to do. A banker would probably look at you strangely and say, "Unsecured loan! What kind of loan is that? You say you want a new business loan, with less than a hundred years of past business history? Sorry!" The one thing they will do is show you the way to the front door.

When working with a venture capitalist, all avenues of investment or deal structuring are possible. Think about any type of investment structure or combination of investments and approach a venture capitalist. Explain your investment and your thought process behind your deal. You might be surprised; it may work.

Never give up. With the right presentation, there is a venture capitalist out there who will fund your deal.

The Small Business Administration (S.B.A.)

I would not do this reference justice, if I didn't mention the S.B.A. loan programs. The purpose of this book is to introduce you to the world of venture capitalists, but in a way, these two worlds are not much different. You still need a good business plan and a good ongoing business. Many newer companies start with the S.B.A., then when larger amounts of capital are needed, they go to a venture capitalist.

I will attempt to give you details on the S.B.A., but their rules change as does the mood of Congress. The phone number of the S.B.A. is listed in the government reference section of this book.

The S.B.A. is an independent government agency created by Congress. The intention of the agency is to help the small business owner obtain a loan and not sell equity (stock), (as a venture capitalist would want), that is partially guaranteed by the agency.

The main focus of the S.B.A. is to help ethnic minorities, women, veterans and other Americans with special needs and circumstances. How the loans are supposed to work are, when you have been turned down by normal means of financing — if you have been refused by banks, venture capitalists or other financing arrangers — then the S.B.A. may step in. Most S.B.A. loans are made through banks, the same banks that may have turned you down the first time. But now the bank has a government agency (S.B.A.) that will guarantee up to 90 percent of your loan.

The last time I checked, the maximum amount was $750,000 that you could obtain through the S.B.A.. The interest is based as an adjustable rate loan that is set to a maximum of up to 2.75 percent above the prime rate. The S.B.A. also has programs for such things as exporting lines of credit, seasonal lines of credit, international trade loans, and community development loans, just to name a few.

There are some cases where the S.B.A. will make direct loans in high unemployment areas, or to some of the aforementioned groups of people. To be eligible for a S.B.A. loan, your company can not be a start-up company (the last time I checked), and they look for companies that are operated for a profit and fall within certain size requirements.

The S.B.A. will not invest in areas like real estate. They like manufacturing companies, wholesaling and distribution companies, service companies, retailing, and construction companies, among others.

There are size limits as to the number of employees and net worth minimums and maximums. There are set guidelines for the amount of sales your company can reach. As I said, it could be worth it to call the S.B.A. as you prepare your business plan to see if there is a possibility of working with them.

Your company's financial strength

Any company that is manufacturing and selling products or services must have the financial strength to conduct business. Did you know almost 70 percent of new companies go out of business within three years? Do you know why such a large percentage of these companies go out of business so soon? Capital, that's all.

Having enough capital is a problem every business owner has to contend with daily. Without enough capital, you are history! You can have the best products or services in the world, but if you run out of money, you are done.

On the average it takes one or two years for some products and service companies to obtain buyer and customer acceptance. This acceptance period can be shortened with some minor changes — minor changes now, but major problems if you wait too long. Having the proper amount of financial backing from the beginning will make your life much easier.

To be a success, your company needs a good product line, financial strength, a professional sales staff and the right presentation of your product. Without these, the buyers from the retail and wholesale trade, and the consumer will be hesitant to purchase your product or service.

How much capital do I ask for?

This is a question that must be considered carefully. Here's why.

Seventy percent of all businesses go broke because the

owner guessed wrong on this question — underestimated, then ran out of money before the business was off and flying.

I must make this statement now, though it will appear again: "Everything takes twice as long to complete, and everything costs twice as much."

Every business owner thinks, as I did myself at one point, that we can save money sometime in the future for what has already been spent. It's just the opposite. Take my word for it. If you have spent more to get established than you imagined you would spend, then it's unlikely you'll be able to play catch up in the future.

So, do **not** try to cut costs when estimating future financial needs to impress your investors. Please do not think that you can make a million dollars with little investment capital. While it may happen — rarely — it does not happen at all as a rule of thumb.

To answer the question I have asked of you is difficult. However, let's put it this way: If you overestimate your costs, you're more likely to succeed in good form.

Questions that you should ask yourself are simple, and these questions may help you better estimate your true costs and revenues.

First, figure the cheapest way for you to establish your future financial needs. Then imagine the very worst case scenario — where everything goes wrong.

After you have these two sets of figures, throw out the cheapest estimate. I know this may sound unprofessional, and not much of an answer to the question, but always remember that 70 percent of all businesses go broke for lack of enough capital to see them through to sunnier days.

If you use my approach to this problem, you also show the investors that you have addressed the worst that can happen. Of course, if you don't use all of the money you've requested, you'll look like a financial wizard in the eyes of your investors. If you do use the additional funds, then you'll have proven your worth in foretelling a future without surprises. In other words, overestimating your financial needs is a win-win situation.

Understanding venture capitalists

Venture capitalists have billions of dollars to invest in companies. A venture capitalist is looking for an exciting company. It does not matter if your company produces consumer products, manufactures chemicals, medical equipment, or is in the service industry. Your company may be established or in its infancy. There are no restrictions on how venture capitalists invest their money. Many venture capitalist invest millions of dollars in companies that have not manufactured any products. Why would a venture capitalist invest millions in your idea?

There is no reason to their logic. Some venture capital firms only want companies that have established track records. Many only want start-up companies. Some do not care if you have been losing money for years. There are no set guidelines or rules a venture capitalist must follow. All they look for is a product or company that has a magnetism like no other. They want something electrifying, something new and different — something that has an excellent chance of creating or expanding in any new or existing market.

The venture capitalists: Who are they, and what are they looking for?

Venture capitalists range from an individual to a company consisting of hundreds of people. You will find an individual who is investing his or her money in as many different ways as the largest venture capitalist.

As a rule of thumb, a venture capitalist company is working with millions of dollars. Most venture capitalist firms' investments range from $250,000 to over $10 million per company. This figure may go as high as $500 million per company. Many times, two or more venture capitalist firms will be in joint venture in any one investment. All venture capitalists have minimum and maximum dollar amounts that they are able to invest in any company, but many times they will have another firm join in with them, if they find an investment they're interested in and the company asking for the investment capital is over their maximum investment limit.

Many venture capitalists set a maximum investment amount but will keep extra investment capital in reserve in case one of their investments needs extra capital due to some unforeseen event.

Where does their money come from? Venture capitalists' money may have been raised through public stock offerings, family trusts, groups of people or company pension funds. This flow of money can come from many different sources. A true venture capitalist is entrusted with the task of finding an investment with the best possible return for their customers or firm.

You will find that some firms invest only in a certain region of the United States or may be limited to only investing in one state. But a large percentage of venture capital firms invest anywhere in the U.S. They also have limitations as to what kind of company in which to invest.

Most firms are looking for high technology or biotechnology investments. But do not be concerned by these big words. A high technology company means any company involved in some type of new sophisticated product. It could be in electronics, computer software, computer hardware, robotics, a new type of rocket ship or other field. Biotechnology investments range from hybrid seeds for crops, to medicine, health care products, health care services, life sciences, or environment products, as a few examples. It is understood by venture capitalists that an investment in these areas will be more risky than an investment in established companies.

Venture capitalists all have their investment areas where they invest capital, and other areas that they will not invest in under any circumstances. The burden of due-diligence falls upon them to seek out and investigate investments. They are entrusted to make investment decisions for their firm or clients with decisions based on facts.

The first of these facts will come from your business plan, so your plan must be as precise as possible. A small fact you may think is not important, may have great importance to the investment capitalist.

Never second guess the investment policies of any venture capitalist or its firms. Everyone has his or her own way of interpreting an investment. The response from identical information given to 50 different venture capitalists will vary as night and day. Some venture capitalists only want companies in their early research and development stage. Others may want only computer software companies. Some may have interests only in companies having many years of losses for tax reasons. The reason for looking for companies with losses may be that with enough capital this old dinosaur may be turned around to make a profit. If the company and profits do turn around, their investment can be sold for more money, or they can take the company public into the stock market and make even more money. Just because a company has lost money for years does not mean there is a lack of interest. For whatever reason a venture capitalist invests in a company, he or she invests because of the possibility of great future profits.

Partners for life

When you start contacting venture capitalists, keep one thought in mind. You must contact as many venture capitalists, or investors of your choice, as necessary until you find the right match — a match that meets both your needs. You and the venture capitalist will be partners for a very long time. You will find that your marriage may be easier to handle than some venture capitalists. Make sure you can manage and work with your choice of partners. When speaking to venture capitalists, ask for names of companies with which they are currently working and investing. Do not be afraid to check their references, as they are sure to check yours. Make certain the venture capitalists have had good working relationships with their past and current partners.

Something new, something different

In your quest for the almighty dollar, keep one thought in mind — the golden rule, *HE WHO HAS THE GOLD, MAKES THE RULES.* This means the person or company investing in your company can make up the rules as they go along. This may not be fair, but it is a way of life.

The quest for money is not an easy one. Your approach and process may be painless or one of the hardest tasks of your life. Hopefully some of my information will enable you to control some of the events during your negotiations with the investment world.

Did you know there are three things that a venture capitalist looks for in any new investment?

Excitement, Excitement and Excitement!

These are the concepts you must project when you are looking for capital. Your company does not have to be on the cutting edge of technology to receive capital. There is capital available for newer, never-before seen products that everyone needs, or a modified product you can manufacture at a lower cost compared to your competition. There are investors who are looking for service companies. No matter what type of company you own, you can obtain capital with the right presentation of your business.

If you had $1 million to invest, what would you look for? A company who may be on the cutting edge of technology may be to your liking. You may want a company that has been established for many years but needs capital to grow. Or you may want a start-up company that only has a good idea and needs money for R & D (research and development). Whatever investment you choose would have to be something exciting to you — a company that seems to draw your attention. If it were not exciting, you would not invest in the company.

Is your deal exciting?

I hope so! If you have a good idea, and your idea is presented properly, you can find a venture capitalist who will fund your deal, but it will depend upon your presentation. Developing your business plan helps you to accomplish this.

You must know your business from the inside out. Developing your company's business plan accomplishes two things. First, you will know every detail concerning your operation. Second, when you are meeting with venture capitalists, you will know all the answers to their questions. The business plan is your foundation for your company. The stronger the foundation, the longer it will stand. The best reason for creating a business plan is for you, the business owner.

What you must project through your business plan

Your company must present itself as knowledgeable, trendsetting and professional — a company that knows where it is, and where it is going. This image can make the difference between your success or failure. If you present any negative impressions from a poorly-written business plan to unproven facts in your plan, your chances of succeeding are not in your favor. Venture capitalists see hundreds of business plans each month. The following is the necessary information you need to prepare before speaking to a venture capitalist. This information must be in the form of a well written business plan. Remember: image, presentation, and excitement will increase your chances of having your request approved.

A business plan is a description of your current business and its proposed future business expansion and profits. It describes your products or services in detail. Facts detailing products and services, marketing concepts, financial requirements, management teams, product research and development (R & D), and cash flow requirements, are just a few of the items needed to describe your business.

A business plan may take weeks or even months to prepare properly. The importance of a well written and believable business proposal will make the difference needed to attract investment capital. Every fact must be as precise as possible. They will check out your facts and figures thoroughly. They will check and recheck your financial needs, production figures, cash flow analysis and other facts you present to them. Do not underestimate their ability to interpret every bit of information you present to them. If they personally do not have the experience to understand the complete concept of your company and its products, they will hire experts who will advise them.

Whether your company is a start-up or an established ten-year-old company, every venture capitalist requires a business plan. This plan must be as complete and precise as possible. But some good advice is to keep your business plan as straightforward and descriptive as possible.

The making of a business plan

There are many ways to assemble a business plan. All business plans, however, contain the same elements. Listed below are twelve areas that you must address in your plan. I would suggest that you keep this format in the order that I have them listed.

1. EXECUTIVE SUMMARY
2. DESCRIPTION OF THE BUSINESS
3. PRODUCT OR SERVICE INFORMATION
4. PRESENT SITUATION
5. OBJECTIVES
6. MANAGEMENT & BOARD OF DIRECTORS
7. PRODUCT RESEARCH AND DEVELOPMENT

8. SALES & MARKETING
9. FUTURE PRODUCTS
10. FINANCIAL PROJECTIONS
11. TESTING AND SUPPORTING DOCUMENTATION
12. FINANCIAL PROPOSAL

Please do not forget to start your business plan with a table of contents.

Executive summary

The first section of your business plan is the executive summary. This will be read by every venture capitalist who reads your business plan. You will find that 90 percent of the venture capitalists will ask you to send this summary to them first. They only want to read this section based on the simple fact of time. If they like what you have written, then they will ask you to send the remaining business plan. You could consider this summary as an advertisement for your company. If you do not grab their attention in this summary, then chances are they will not ask for or read the remaining 90 percent of your business plan. This section should be between three and five pages long. You want the venture capitalist to be able to read and understand your company's concepts and intentions in less than five minutes of reading time. Summarizing and encapsulating your entire business is your goal. But the ultimate goal is to get their attention so they will want to investigate your company further. This may not be an easy task, but this is how the system works. Five pages may not, in your mind, explain your entire company, but that's all with which you have to work. This executive summary should outline each of the 12 sections listed above. Take the highlights from each section and work with these facts only. All of your supporting documentation will be in the remaining 90 percent of the business plan.

Do not underestimate the importance of this section. Be focused and clear in demonstrating your overall goals with precise clarity and a no-nonsense approach. In the last one or two paragraphs of your summary you need to summarize your financial requirements. Describe the capital you are requesting and the profits that the venture capitalist should receive in return. This section must be as brief as possible. You do not want to back yourself into a corner by asking for too much, thus giving the appearance that you are not flexible. Remember, you want to get their attention so they will want to continue talking with you.

Description of the business

This section explains the precise nature of your business and its history. The first paragraph or two will outline the products or services you sell and who your customers are. Outline your competition and why your company stands out in the forefront of its field. Do not go into great detail about the competition; you will go into greater detail in the following section on "subject."

In these first few lines you must grab the attention of your reader. Tell the reader why you think this company will be one of the best in the business. Why there is a need for this company and the future as you see it. Try to explain some of the future economic forecasts showing that your company has great growth potential. Detail the reasons behind the decisions that led you to believe you could have a thriving company — a company that is better than all others.

The other facts in this section should include the purpose of your company, its history, general description of products or services, and benefits. It would be a good idea to inform the reader of the business environment as you see it today. Go into detail on the industry, regulatory problems (if any), and, of course, an overview of the entire market with which you compete.

Here are questions for you to address in your business plan:

- Where does your company stand as of today, or what stage of development are you in?
- Are you in an R & D stage?
- Are you a start-up company?
- Are you an established company with years of operating history? Just explain the facts that pertain to your status at this point in time.

Also you need to explain what your company does:

- Do you manufacture consumer products, industrial products?
- Are you a service company, a retail company?
- Whatever you manufacture, sell or service should be explained here.

Provide a history of your company:

- Why you started the company.
- The reason you wanted to start your company.
- Any information on your past experience and why you thought of this company.
- What is the status of ownership of your company.
- Are you a corporation? If you are a corporation, are you a C corp or a S corp?
- Minority owned?
- Sole proprietor?
- Partnership?
- Limited partnership?
- Woman owned?

The facts pertaining to description of your company must get the attention of the reader.

Product or service information

In this section you will discuss the outstanding characteristics of your products or services. This is when you obviously pat yourself on the back describing just how good your idea and company is, and how well your idea is needed in the marketplace. In complete detail, be specific and as precise in the explanation of your product or service as you can. Describe how your product works and the advantage of your product or service over the competition. Explain the advantages of your product or service, showing that your company has something the public needs or is waiting for. Do not get overly enthusiastic, but keep your comments and thoughts as straightforward as possible. Yes, you want to get their attention, but be realistic throughout your business plan. Remember, venture capitalists see hundreds of business plans per month, and they can tell if you know what you are doing within the first few sections of your business plan.

Answers to questions in this section would include: Will your customers save money with the use of your products? Is service better than your competitors? These are good questions, and you must be able to answer them to satisfy the venture capitalist. In this section try to describe each product or service with which you are engaged by listing special features, advantages and benefits of your company. Are the products patented or licensed, or do you have to pay any royalties?

These questions on exact details on your products or services should be addressed in this section:

- Are your products or service the best you can find?
- Why are they best?
- Or how can they be the best?
- What are the benefits your company has over its competition?
- Have you defined your market segment?
- Why is there a need for your business or service?
- How does your company differ from the competition?
- Does your product or service save time and/or money?

I would also go into any detailed information as to whether

your product needs to be patented, or if you have already patented your product. Thought should be given as to whether you should trademark your product name or service name or logo. Does your company have a secret formula that you may not want to patent? Do you have to copyright any computer software or printed information? These questions should be discussed with your attorney. Another aspect that you must ask your attorney is whether you need the venture capitalist to sign a nondisclosure agreement. If you have not patented your product or trademarked your name or logo, you may want this form signed before you send your business plan to a venture capitalist. This form is for your protection. If you have trade secrets that you must protect, then have the firm sign this agreement.

Present situation

The current situation of your company as of this point in time is explained in this section. State the exact circumstances of your company ranging from where you are located to the names of some of your customers. This section is where the venture capitalist will start to determine if they are still interested in reading the remainder of your business plan. No matter how good or bad you think the state of your company is, let the venture capitalist decide for himself or herself. If you are working out of your basement, then state so. There is nothing wrong with working out of your basement or garage. One of the richest men in the computer world started this way. Just make the facts known where your company stands today. Here are some questions that you must answer if they apply to your company.

- Have you completed your R & D?
- If not, how far along are you?
- How long will you need until you are completed with the R & D process?
- Where is your company located?
- Are you working out of your home?

- Are you leasing office or warehouse space?
- What are you paying in rent?
- How long is your lease?
- Are you running out of space at your current address?

Where are you currently working or producing your products:

- Are you producing products at this time?
- If so, what is your production?

Who are you selling your products or services to:

- Who are your customers?
- Are any of them on the fortune 500 list?
- Do you have business relationships or references?

Are you producing your own products, or do you use outside vendors to assemble your products:

- Are you carrying inventory?
- Are you running out of inventory?
- Who are your suppliers and vendors?
- Do you depend on special suppliers to produce your products?

How is your quality control system:

- How is the inspection handled?
- Who has the authority to reject products that do not meet your product guidelines?
- Do you have a vendor quality assurance inspection system in place?

How is your current financial status:

- Are you making money?
- Are you having trouble meeting payroll?
- Do you have existing loans?
- If so, are they paid on time?
- Are you out of money?

Here in this section is where you must be honest. No

one in this venture capital field likes any surprises.

Do you need special equipment to manufacture your products or services:

- Do you have this equipment?
- Is this equipment available to purchase?
- Is this equipment new or high technology?
- Do you know if and when you can purchase this equipment?

I hope I did not overwhelm you with this last section, but this section is of great importance. A venture capitalist can determine if your company is ready for capital, or if more R & D is required before they will consider an investment in your company.

There is a very important fact to remember throughout your quest for capital. The further along you are in R & D, the greater your production is; the more customers you have, and the more established your company is, the better off you will be!

Objectives

The objectives section will go over some of the same details as listed above. The only difference here is what exactly are your goals from this point forward for your company. After the capital is in place, where do you foresee your company five years down the road. Explaining how you intend to make their investment grow and expand will be of great importance.

Start this section stating your goals and objectives, then go into detail:

- Do you plan on moving into an office/warehouse?
- Can your current plant or office space handle future growth?
- Do you need another warehouse with loading docks?
- Do you need easy access to highways, railroads or airports?

- If you have a current lease, can you terminate your lease, if you must move?
- Will your production system change with expanded growth?
- Do you need more automated equipment?
- What kind of equipment is needed?

Will you need other office equipment:

- How will you pay for any new plant or equipment with proceeds of venture capital or future profits?

Will you need to expand or hire additional labor and top personnel:

- Is there the personnel or employee base in your community that fits your needs?

What and where is your market going to be over the next five years:

- How will your market share grow with current products?
- What do you envision for future products or services? (You will go into greater detail on future products or services in a later section.)

Will your inventory grow and by how much:

- Will you need other shipping or manufacturing facilities in other parts of the U.S.?

Everyone likes to see a great future in any company. The better your future looks, the better deal you can make with the venture capitalist.

Management and Board of Directors

Venture capitalists look for expertise in the management team of any possible investment. The founders or owners of any company must be completely knowledgeable of every aspect of their business. As an example, if your company is established, chances are you have experienced personnel. From the president of the company through your key personnel, you need their full background history and a current resumé. The question will be: Do the owners have experience in managing any companies?

Who makes up your current management team:

- President?
- Vice president?
- Secretary?
- Comptroller?
- Sales manager?
- Manufacturing manager?
- Top department personnel?

Who is on your staff as an outside consultant:

- Legal?
- Marketing consultant?
- Accounting C.P.A.?
- Advertising consultant?

List your Board of Directors:

- Chairman?
- Vice chairman?
- And all directors?

If you do not have these people associated with your company, how will you attract them? Where are you going to get them? The management team and its associates are as important as the products or services you have. Without the proper management, staff, and consultants, if needed, you're in for trouble.

For an example, in start-up companies many of the top personnel have excellent research and development backgrounds but no management experience. If this is the case, you need to have a top-notch management team on your side.

The management team of any company will be of great importance and a big topic to decide before venture capitalists invest their money. This management team will be scrutinized by the venture capitalists. You need to surround yourself with personnel having the areas of expertise you lack. Do not take this view the wrong way. It would be better for you to find a top management person to run the day-to-day operations of your company before the venture capitalists suggest one for you. Find the person with whom you can work. Remember, the better management team you assemble before the venture capitalist invests, the better deal you may make for your company.

I do not want to alarm you about your management team or your board of directors at this time. If you are looking for smaller investment amounts through venture capitalists we must keep some things in perspective. If you are looking for $10,000 to $100,000, no one expects to see the past president of G. M. as your president or chairman of the board of directors. The point I am trying to emphasize: surround yourself with the personnel that rounds out your management team. You may have a retired personal friend who was in management in the past. Your accountant may consider being on your board, or he may be your accountant and comptroller of the company. Try to assemble a group of people who can help you as you look for the capital you need. Their input and suggestions may be very helpful to you and your company.

The larger the amount of capital you are seeking creates a greater need for professional experienced personnel. This includes your board of directors and your overall management team.

To sum up this section, you want to show any investor that you have the skills and expertise to know when and where you need professional help or guidance. Remember, you are an entrepreneur, and you are intelligent enough to realize when you need help. This will be apparent to the venture capitalists, and they will appreciate working with you.

Product research and development (R & D)

A venture capitalist will put your company through the ringer when it comes to your research and development (R&D). No matter if you are looking for $10,000 or $25 million, the proof must be on the table. Remember your nondisclosure form to make sure you are also protected.

The information you must supply to the venture capitalist includes everything from A to Z. Do not hold back any details that could affect the decision of the venture capitalist. You must give them all pertinent information regarding your total business. Proof from outside laboratories will go a long way toward proving your products work as intended. Listing the names of experts in your field of business, who may be able to substantiate your claims, will not hurt at all. Experts, who can give supporting technical and engineering information that confirms all of your claims and statements, are very important to use and have available for future questions and problems.

Because of the different types of businesses purchasing this reference book, I can think of thousands of questions that could be asked. However, it would be impossible to go into detail and provide all the information necessary to answer every question a venture capitalist might ask concerning your R & D, although you can be assured you can never give a venture capitalist enough information. The more complex your product or service, the more information you will need. This is why you must have complete detailed information on all R & D.

Here are some of the questions that should be discussed in this section:

- Is the competition looking at some of the same ideas you are?
- Is the technology so advanced that there may be un-

known questions that may affect our company?
- Can these questions be solved if problems arise?
- Is your technology staff the best in the business?
- Do they have enough background in this technology?
- Are they good problem solvers?
- Are you on the cutting edge of breakthrough technology?
- If so, Why?
- How far ahead of the competition do you think you are?
- How long would it take for another company to catch up to your technology?
- Where can you take this technology from here?
- Are there any potential side effects with any processing of your products?
- Are there any hazardous waste by-products related to the production?
- Are there any disposal problems associated with the manufacturing of your products?
- Are there any government regulations that you must contend with? If so, are these state or federal regulations?
- Are there any past companies that have failed with the same technology that you are pursuing?
- If so, how does your research differ from theirs?

You will need extensive research and documentation detailing the performance, reliability and quality of the product.

Sales and marketing

The distribution and sales is just another factor that will be of great importance to any venture capitalist. In this section, I will spend more time explaining the sales and marketing of your company.

Who is going to sell your products? And who do you think will buy your products? Market research must be as complete as possible. The biggest question will be: Is there a market for this great idea? You must have all of the answers before you approach a venture capitalist, and, again, developing your business proposal helps you to accomplish this.

This next section shows you the steps needed to complete your sales and marketing approach. If you have a start-up company, then this section's information is needed to start planning your sales force. If you have a current company, this information might help you increase your sales. By increasing your sales, the venture capitalist will not see as much at risk, thus asking for less ownership. Questions you must ask yourself are the same the venture capitalist will ask if you are producing consumer products.

How do I get my products into:

- 10,000 Computer and Software Stores?
- 150,000 Grocery Stores?
- 500,000 Manufacturing Companies?
- 56,000 Drug Stores?
- 200,000 Wholesalers?
- 122,000 Gift Shops?
- 45,000 Hardware Stores?
- 26,000 Department Stores?
- 35,000 Toy and Hobby Stores?
- 11,000 Health Food Stores?
- 27,000 Sporting Goods Stores?
- The U.S. Military?
- U.S. and Local Governments?
- And 1000s of chain stores?

And the list goes on and on.

You could hire twenty or thirty sales people and have them travel to all corners of the United States. But the venture capitalists would like you to take a better, less costly approach. There is a way to make your life easier, give you the sales needed to survive and impress the venture capitalist, all at the same time. Since successful marketing is the business owner's ultimate goal, both sides of the coin must be examined. As I explain the facts needed in your business plan, here is a list of a few questions to think about as you read on:

The first question is to explain your market, and what is so unique about your company's products or services.

What does your business customer base look like:
- Type of customer?
- Type of business using your product or service?
- Size of your customer base? (Are they Fortune 500 companies or smaller companies?)

If your customer is the public, then:
- Type of consumer?
- Age?
- Sex?
- Family size?
- Income average?
- Occupation?
- Education?

How will you sell your products or services:
- Outside sales staff?
- Inside sales staff?
- Will you use manufacture sales reps?
- How many sales employees do you currently have? How many will you need over the next five years?

What is your current or expected means of distribution:
- Salespeople?
- Mail order?
- Dealers?
- Franchising?

Will you use your own sales staff or sales reps for your

outside sales representation:

- What will be their commissions?
- What will be their territories?
- What will be their salary or pay scale?

What is your target market:

- How will you promote your company's products or services, how does your competition promote their products or services, who will promote your company?
- Will you use outside consultants?

Will you advertise through:

- Newspapers?
- T.V.?
- Radio?
- Magazines?
- How much will you expect to spend on advertising?

What are your sales goals for the next five years:

- How will you start or expand your sales volume?
- Will you expand into other geographical areas?

What is your expected share of the market:

- How will you increase your share?
- How much will your share of the market increase over the next five years?
- How will your current competitors lose their market share to you and for what reasons?

How do you set your prices:

- Have your prices been stable?
- Are you dependent on any materials that may affect your prices such as gold or other precise ingredients?
- What are your profit margins?
- How will they differ over the next years?

We all know a company needs sales to survive. Establishing a national sales organization is important to any company. The travel cost associated with an in-house sales staff, such as airplanes, hotels and car rentals can cost a fortune. The expense of a sales call is estimated between $250 to $500 per appointment. With the number of sales people needed to cover the country, this would cost a large fortune. But the sooner you have a national sales organization, the sooner you have sales. This brings up all types of problems for any business owner. And you want to keep your sales costs as low as possible. But there are other questions that will be asked about your sales and marketing plan. Can your sales staff walk into Sears, Rite-Aid, Wal-Mart or any of the other thousands of retailers and wholesalers, and sell your products? If you have an existing sales force, you may have been trying to establish these contacts for some time. This brings up other important questions. How do I get in the front door, present my products and have them sold? This question will be asked by the venture capitalist. Also, how do I do this without spending a fortune? The answers to these questions are very easy. They're called manufacturer sales representatives. My other reference book, ***Let The Pros Sell It,*** goes into detail on manufacturers' sales representatives.

We live and work in a very competitive society. Therefore, you must have an effective and professional approach that is superior to your competitors. You need the expertise of manufacturer sales representatives. Why? There are many reasons to use these professionals. The best reason is an existing relationship with every major national chain and wholesaler in the United States. Your company can have an established professional, first rate sales organization within weeks. Sales reps have the strengths and the knowledge where you may have the weaknesses. Why reinvent the wheel? A professional sales organization with proven sales expertise and no expense, until your products are sold, is the best of all worlds.

If your company is established, the use of sales reps could

be very helpful to you. If you need capital, investors look very closely at certain points. Most of all, they are interested in sales and potential sales orders. Think of what you need to survive — it's sales! Anyone thinking about investing or lending capital wants to see orders. It, then, becomes important for venture capitalists to see a professional sales organization — a sales organization that has the ability to get purchase orders. From a financial point of view, when you have purchase orders, everything looks better.

Future products

A venture capitalist wants to see the possibilities of new products for the future. A one-product company does not have great appeal. Remember, the venture capitalist wants excitement. Do you need working prototypes of future products? No, but ideas with some background information can go a long way. If you can produce a drawing or two of any upcoming or future products, all the better. Give them something to look forward to.

When you talk about upcoming products or a new generation of your current products or services, describe why you think they would be better. How far away is your future products or new generation of products? Explain if the R & D of the ideas will be hard to develop, or is the technology available at this point in time. Will your current products have a limited life cycle, or will the business environment in later years create a greater demand for your company's products.

Questions to be addressed in this section should be:

- Are the new products a new generation of your current products or services, or completely new ideas?
- What type of products do you envision for the future?
- Will you be developing products outside your area of expertise?
- Will you need other research personnel to develop these new ideas? How will the R & D be paid for?

- How long will the R & D take until you have working prototypes and products to sell?

I know there may be a lot of questions in this section, but do your best. You probably have your hands full of problems pertaining to your current products or services, let alone thinking of new products. But, to repeat myself, a one-product company may not be the best investment for any venture capitalist. Yet there are some very successful one-product companies in the world.

Financial information and projections

There is one fact that I must bring to your attention, and please give this thought a great deal of attention. All venture capitalists look at your expectations, estimates, time lines and figures, and almost double them, if they are not satisfied with your financial estimates. I am not saying you are misleading them, but it is an understood fact that, as I said before, "Everything takes twice as long, and everything costs twice as much." And profits will be half of what the excited business owner thinks. This fact is true for most newer companies.

Things happen in every new company that you cannot expect. Delays, cost overruns, personnel problems, you name it, and it can happen. This is why, when speaking to venture capitalists, let them know what potential problems may arise. The more upfront you are with them, the better chance you have in getting your capital. This section must include information pertaining to the financial history of the company. Where did you get the capital to start your company? How much capital have you put into the company over the years? What is your current financial position?

You will have to go into detail on revenue projections and expenses for the next five years. I would like to say something at this time about estimating your growth and expenses for the next five years. This may be very hard for you to accomplish. If you can estimate the next two or three years with better accuracy, then use the shorter time estimates. Other facts must include all credit arrangements with your suppliers as well as your customers. Check and recheck your budgets to make sure you are not missing any information. You must mention if you have any contingent liabilities or any tax problems or special considerations.

In this section you need to have current and estimated financial statements. The estimated financial statements should go out for five years, if possible. I would suggest having your accountant or a financial analyst help in the preparation of these projections.

- What are your assets?
- What are your liabilities?
- Current cash flow?
- Current profit and loss statement?
- Current balance sheet?

Now repeat this information as a projection for the next five years.

As far as your current cash flow analysis is concerned, be sure to include receivables you carry for:

- 30 days?
- 60 days?
- 90 days?
- Over 120 days?

How much capital do you need for the next two to three years:

- For what will the investment capital be used?
- Do you have current loans?
- Will these loans be paid off with the venture capital?
- Have any of the owners signed personally on these loans?

Are your sales a seasonal business:

- How will you get by when your sales slow down for

that period of the year?

The other information you should list is who are you banking with at this time. Give the venture capitalist your current personal financial statement and those of any large shareholders.

Also list when your company updates its financial records — monthly, quarterly or annually. May I recommend that you update your records each quarter for the first year or two in business? This way you can keep greater control over your expenses.

The last statement will be when your company will arrive at a break-even point. That is, in the black — profitable! This statement will be of importance to everyone.

Testing and supporting documentation

This last section will show your supporting documentation backing all of your claims. Outside laboratory reports and testimony from outside experts or users of your products would be very helpful in this section. This section is the same as your R & D section, but here is where you will put copies of all your testing, research, and laboratory results. Any statements from experts and outside testing should also be supplied here.

Financial proposal

Prepare your proposal asking for the capital needs of your company. Be very realistic in your proposal. Summarize all the facts that I have mentioned throughout this book. Initially, try not to be too specific in your request. Whatever you are seeking, as far as capital, can and will be changed during the negotiations. Try to be firm in your approach, but whatever you are asking for will be negotiated and changed many times.

Remember, you are dealing with deal makers — people who make the impossible deals work, deals that banks would never consider. They take risks that most people would never try.

Stating your proposal first will solidify your stand and show evidence of your intentions. For your information, approximately 95 percent of the investments from venture capitalists are not loans. The venture capitalists want an equity ownership (stock) in your company. This does not mean however, that they might not rule out some type of loan to your company. When you work with a venture capitalist, remember you can create any type of deal. All avenues of deal making are open. Use them wisely.

Think about one possibility — if you were to do better than you and the venture capitalist thought. If you were to make more money, develop more products, then you may want to ask for some of your stock back. This should be thought about if you are a start-up company. If you are a start-up, then you will give a larger percentage of ownership to the venture capitalist. Remember, the farther along you are in your company and the more established your company is, the less ownership will be asked for by the venture capitalists.

Also, consider the fact (upfront) of the possibility that you and the venture capitalist cannot get along at a later date. Consider an agreement that you may need down the road. Not every marriage or partnership works. There is always a possibility that you and the venture capitalists cannot see eye-to-eye, and you may want them out of your life, or the same is possible for them. You may want to have a buy-out or buy-back provision if things go better than expected, or you are no longer able to work with the venture capitalists. This is just a thought for you to consider. Take time thinking about this matter.

The information needed in this final section of your business plan is what amount of capital is needed by the company. You have to ask for an amount of capital and what you will give up in ownership for the investment. You need to tell the venture capitalist how and when you need the capital. You may not need all the capital at one time. You may need 50 percent now and the other 50 percent in a year. You may need an amount of capital now, but you do not know if you might need more money at a later date. If your company grows faster than you thought, you may need more capital. If this is a possibility, then ask the venture capitalist for the possibility of a future loan or for them to buy more stock in your company.

State all of your financing requirements in your proposal. State the amount of capital needed and the purpose for the capital. In a few pages I will explain one of my situations with one investment that I made — they bought a Mercedes Benz automobile! Any capital you receive from the venture capitalist must go for the reason you stated the capital was intended.

One last note on this subject. The venture capitalist will want a few seats on the board of directors. Offer this up front along with your funding request.

What do I need to send to a venture capitalist?

There is a format and a proper procedure to follow when you present a business plan to a venture capitalist. I would first send your executive summary to the venture capitalist and not your total business plan. If the venture capitalists want your complete business plan, they will call or write. Again, I would not send a full copy of your business plan, unless the venture capitalist has an interest in your company. The less amount of information out on the street, i.e. your business plan, the less chance your information will wind up in your competitors' hands. You may think this is a small, non-important fact, but it is important. Never let your competition know what and where you stand in your company at any time.

In closing

Venture capitalists are approached every day of the week. I can't tell you how many times I have been approached in a restaurant or shopping mall with the greatest deal in the world. People with money are approached every day to make loans or investments. We look at deal after deal all the time.

When I fund a new company, many thoughts enter my mind. Are these people honest? Do they have a product that makes a difference? Do I think they will waste the money? Will they want a new Mercedes Benz with the money I gave them? Don't laugh; this happened to one company in which I invested. The first thing they bought was a new Benz. Needless to say, I was not a happy camper.

These questions must be answered in the mind of a venture capitalist. Consider if you were on the other side of the table: Would you make the investment, if you had the money? If you can honestly say, "Yes," to this question, then you have a very good chance of obtaining the capital you need.

The last bit of information you need is bookkeeping. From the very start of your company, be sure to keep excellent records. Hire a C.P.A. to maintain audited financial records. This becomes very important, if your company intends to go public some time down the road. It is extremely expensive to recreate your old financial records from years' past.

How do I use this reference guide?

The million dollar question! The information you have assembled should be neatly typed and bound. A presentation that looks good and flows smoothly will help immensely. When you use this reference guide, you will find the name of the venture capital firms, addresses, phone numbers, the region of the U.S. in which they invest, and the area of investment in which they specialize. Also, I have tried to list the areas of investment in which the venture capitalists do not want to invest. Many venture capitalists are open to many areas of lending. This is noted in the reference guide.

I would not pick up the phone and call a venture capitalist at this time. I would suggest that you write a letter of introduction and send it with a copy of the executive summary. A venture capitalist would rather see an executive summary than your entire business plan. The reason for sending a summary is very simple. Some venture capital firms may work on only ten or twenty projects at a time. Some lend only a maximum amount of money each month, quarter, or year. They may not be able to work with you for months. This is why I suggest sending only an executive summary. They will call, if they have an interest in your company.

Do not give confidential information in your letter. You do not want to give your secrets away. Protect yourself but give just enough information to get their attention. Remember one very important fact when writing your executive summary: *excitement, excitement, and excitement!*

When you send your executive summary, send a self-addressed stamped return envelope. This makes it easier for the venture capitalist to respond to your summary. When you get a positive response, then you will need to have your non-disclosure form prepared to be signed by the venture capitalists and their firm, if you and your lawyer think it is necessary.

Never give any money to a so-called venture capitalist; no upfront fees or deposits

This has been known to happen many, many times: Some so-called venture capital firms ask you to give them a good-faith deposit. Why? Good question! There is no reason in the world why a venture capitalist needs a large sum of money upfront. There have been scams over the years where the so-called venture capitalist asked for a deposit to review your information. Some costs may be realistic and justified, but these are few and far between. I have seen so-called venture capitalists ask for $10,000 to over $100,000 in good faith deposits. I will guarantee the only probable outcome from this deposit will be the loss of your money. Some of the excuses for deposits are:

-Lawyer fees,

-Accounting review fees,

-Travel expenses,

-Document review fees,

-Office overhead fees,

-Research fees,

or the best one of all, "Our funding source is out of the country. We need you to pay for all the phone calls, faxes and travel costs to see our money partners who are out of the country."

THERE IS NO EXCUSE FOR ANY UPFRONT FEES, NO MATTER HOW GOOD A REASON.

Mergers, acquisitions, buy-outs, turnarounds and special situations

For any situation as:

1. MERGERS AND ACQUISITIONS,
2. MANAGEMENT & EMPLOYEE BUY-OUTS,
3. TURNAROUNDS,
4. SPECIAL SITUATIONS

you will need to work with the larger venture capitalists. You will be able to know who these are by the minimum dollars amounts they invest. For any of these situations listed above, I would suggest calling the venture capital firm to see if they have interest in these situations only. Since deals of this nature are more complex and harder to complete, not all venture capitalists will take on this type of project.

Do not forget to obtain your bar code

A bar code can be obtained by calling 513-435-3870 or writing to Uniform Code Council, Inc., 8163 Old Yankee Rd., Suite J, Dayton, OH 45458

The information contained within the reference guide portion of this book is deemed reliable. HUTTON Financial Services Corp., Inc. has made careful attempts to verify the accuracy of the information contained therein, ***HOWEVER, ITS ACCURACY IS NOT GUARANTEED.***

Federal Agencies and National Trade Associations

FEDERAL AGENCIES AND NATIONAL TRADE ASSOCIATIONS

THAT MAY HAVE HELPFUL ADVICE FOR YOUR COMPANY.

Federal Agencies

Bureau of Export Administration
P.O. Box 273
Washington, D.C.
202-482-4811

Consumer Product Safety Commission
Washington, D.C. 20207
301-504-0580

Dept. of Commerce
14th & Constitution Ave. NW
Washington, D.C. 20230
202-482-2000

Economic Development Administration
14th & Constitution Ave. NW, Room 7828
Washington, D.C. 20230
202-482-5112

Employment & Training Administration
200 Constitution Ave. NW
Washington, D.C. 20210
202-219-6871

Environmental Protection Agency
401 M. St. SW
Washington, D.C. 20460
202-260-4454

Federal Communications Commission
1919 M. St. NW
Washington D.C. 20554
202-632-7000

Federal Trade Commission
6th & Pennsyl. Ave., NW
Washington, D.C. 20580
202-418-0200

Food and Drug Administration
5600 Fishers Lane
Rockville, MD 20857
301-443-3170

Immigration and Naturalization Service
425 I St. NW
Washington, D.C. 20536
1-800-755-0777

Interstate Commerce Commission
12th St. & Constitution, Ave. NW
Washington, D.C. 20423
202-927-7600

National Credit Union Administration
1775 Duke St.
Alexandria, VA 22314
703-518-6300

National Labor Relations Board
1099 14th St. NW
Washington, D.C. 20570
202-273-1000

National Transportation Safety Board
490 L'Enfant Plaza, SW
Washington, D.C. 20594
202-382-6600

Occupational Safety and Health Administration
200 Constitution Ave. NW
Washington, D.C. 20210
202-219-8148

Patent & Trademark Office
Washington, D.C. 20231
703-308-4357
703-557-4636

Sm. Business Administration
409 3rd St. SW
Washington, D.C. 20416
202-205-7717
202-205-7701
1-800-827-5722

Small Business Export & Import Bank
Washington, D.C.
1-800-565-3946

United States International Trade Commission
500 E St. SW
Washington, D.C. 20436
202-205-2000

Veterans Employment & Training Service
200 Constitution Ave. NW
Washington, D.C. 20210
202-219-9116

Employment & Training Administration
200 Constitution Ave. NW
Washington, D.C. 20210
202-219-6871

National Trade Associations

AMERICAN ELECTRONICS ASSOC.
5201 Great America Parkway
Santa Clara, CA 95054
408-987-4200

AMERICAN HARDWARE MANUFACTURERS ASSOC.
801 N. Plaza Drive
Schaumburg, IL 60173
708-605-1025

AMERICAN HEALTH CARE ASSOC.
1201 L. St. NW
Washington, D.C. 20005
202-842-4444

AMERICAN HEALTH & BEAUTY AIDS
401 N. Michigan Ave.
Chicago, IL 60611
312-644-6610

AUTOMOTIVE SERVICE INDUSTRY ASSOC.
25 N.W. Point Blvd. Suite 425
Elk Grove Village, IL 60007
708-228-1310

COSMETIC TOILETRY & FRAGRANCE ASSOC.
1101 17th St. N.W. Suite 300
Washington, DC 20036
202-331-1770

DIRECT MARKETING ASSOC.
1101 17th St. NW #705
Washington D.C. 20036
202-347-1222

ELECTRONICS INDUSTRIES ASSOC.
2500 Wilson Blvd.
Arlington, VA 22201
703-907-7500

FOOD MARKETING INSTITUTE
800 Connecticut Ave. NW #400
Washington, DC 20006
202-452-8444

HEALTH INDUSTRY MANUFACTURERS ASSOC.
1200 G. St. NW #400
Washington, D.C. 20005
202-783-8700

INFORMATION INDUSTRY ASSOC.
555 New Jersey Ave. #800
Washington D.C. 20001
202-639-8260

INFORMATION TECHNOLOGY ASSOC. OF AMERICA
1616 N. Fort Meyer Dr. #1300
Arlington, VA 22209
703-522-5055

INFORMATION TECHNOLOGY INDUSTRY COUNSEL
1250 I St. NW Suite 200
Washington, D.C. 20005
202-737-8888

INTERNATIONAL MASS RETAIL ASSOC.
1901 Pennsylvania Ave., N.W.
Washington, DC 20006
202-861-0774

NATIONAL ASSOC. OF ENVIRONMENTAL PROFESSIONALS
5165 MacArthar Blvd.
Washington D.C. 20016
202-966-1500

NATIONAL ASSOC. OF RETAIL DRUGGIST
205 Daingerfield Rd.
Alexandria. VA 22314
703-683-8200

NATIONAL ASSOC. OF DRUG STORES
413 N. Lee St
Alexandria, VA 22313
703-549-3001

NATIONAL HOUSEWARES MANUFACTURERS ASSOC.
6400 Shafer Ct.
Rosemont, IL 60018
708-292-4200

PRIVATE LABEL MANUFACTURERS ASSOC.
369 Lexington Ave., 3rd Floor
New York, NY 10017
212-972-3131

SCHOOL & HOME OFFICE ASSOC.
3055 Kettering Blvd. Suite 401
Dayton, OH 45439
513-297-2250

State Economic and Development Agencies

State Economic and Development Agencies

The information contained within the reference guide portion of this book is deemed reliable. HUTTON Financial Services Corp., Inc. has made careful attempts to verify the accuracy of the information contained therein, ***HOWEVER, ITS ACCURACY IS NOT GUARANTEED.***

STATE AGENCIES AND DEVELOPMENT PROGRAMS

You may want to check with the state your company is located in for many reasons. Many states have economic development agencies to help employers and companies exist in their state. They try to promote business within the state with many programs which you may take advantage of. They have information on tax breaks, incentives, training new personnel programs, special minority programs, and many other services. Some states have funds to invest in companies. Others have free trade zones that you may take advantage of or incubators. (An incubator is a large building where the state or county will help your company — from paying your rent to answering the phone.) There are economic block grants some states issue every year along with many different training programs. Some of these programs may pay up to 50 percent of the hourly pay for some of your employees. You may find many other programs to your liking, so please call your state or development agency to see if they have any programs that fit your needs.

You may want to check with each state agency to inquire if your county has any special programs.

ALABAMA
Alabama Development
Office
401 Adams Ave.
Montgomery, AL, 36103
205-242-0400

ALABAMA
Small Business
Development Center
University of Alabama at
Birmingham
Medical Towers Building
1717 11st Ave., Suite 419
Birmingham, AL 35294
205-934-7260

ALASKA
Alaska Division of Economic Development
P. O. Box 110804
Juneau, AK 99811-0804
907-465-2017

ALASKA
Small Business Development Center
University of Alaska Anchorage
430 W. Seventh Ave., Suite 110
Anchorage, AK 99501
907-274-7232

ARIZONA
Arizona Business Connection
c/o Commerce Dept
3800 N. Central Ave #1500
Phoenix, Az 85012
602-280-1480

ARIZONA
Small Business Development Center
2411 West 14th St. Suite 132
Tempe, AZ 85281
602-731-8720

ARKANSAS
Arkansas Industrial Development Commission Of Arkansas
#1 Capital Mall
Little Rock, AR 72201
501-682-2052

ARKANSAS
Small Business Development Center
University of Arkansas at Little Rock
100 South Main, Suite 401
Little Rock, AR 72201
501-324-9043

CALIFORNIA
California Trade and Commerce
801 K St. #1600
Sacramento, CA 95814
916-322-1394

CALIFORNIA
Small Business Development Center
801 K St. Suite 1700
Sacramento, CA 95814
916-324-5068

COLORADO
Colorado Office of Economic Development
1625 Broadway #1710
Denver, CO 80202
303-892-3840

COLORADO
Small Business Development Center
1625 Broadway, Suite 1710
Denver, CO 80202
303-892-3809

CONNECTICUT
Connecticut Business
Response Center Dept. of
Economic Development
865 Brook St.
Rocky Hill, CT 06067
1800-392-2122

CONNECTICUT
Small Business
Development Center
University of Connecticut
2 Bourn Place, U-94
Stoers, CT 06269
203-486-4135

DELAWARE
Delaware Economic
Development Office
99 Kings Hwy.
Dover, DE 19901
302-739-4271

DELAWARE
Small Business
Development Center
University of Delaware
Purnell Hall, Suite 005
Newark, DE 19716-2711
302-831-2747

DISTRICT OF COLUMBIA (WASHINGTON, D.C.)
Washington D.C. Office of
Economic Development
717 14th St. NW, 12th Floor
Washington, D.C. 20005
202-727-6600

DISTRICT OF COLUMBIA
Small Business
Development Center
Howard University
6th and Fairmont St. NW
Room 128
Washington, DC 20059
202-806-1550

FLORIDA
Florida Economic
Development Office
107 W. Gaines St.
Tallahassee, FL 32399-2000
904-488-6300

FLORIDA
Small Business
Development Center
University of
West Florida
11000 University Parkway
Bldg. #8
Pensacola, FL 32514
904-474-2908

GEORGIA
Georgia Department of
Industry and Trade
& Economic Develop.
285 Peachtree Center Ave.
Suite 1100
Atlanta, Ga 30303
404-656-3573

GEORGIA
Small Business
Development Center
University of Georgia
Chicopee Complex, 1180 East
Broad St.
Athens, GA 30602-5412
706-542-7436

HAWAII
Hawaii Economic
Development Board
P.O. Box 2359
Honolulu, HI 96804
808-586-2363

HAWAII
Small Business
Development Center
University of Hawaii at Hilo
523 W. Lanikaula St.
Hilo, HI 96720
808-933-3515

IDAHO
Idaho Department of
Commerce
700 W. State St.
Boise ID 83720-0093
208-334-2470

IDAHO
Small Business
Development Center
Boise State University
1910 University Drive #ISBDC
Boise, ID 83725
208-385-1640

ILLINOIS
Illinois Commerce of
Community Affaire
620 E Adams
Springfield, IL 62701
217-782-7500

ILLINOIS
Small Business
Development Center
Department of Commerce &
Community Affairs
620 East Adams St., 6th Floor
Springfield, IL 62701
217-524-5856

INDIANA
Indiana Business
Development Division
1 N. Capital #700
Indianapolis, IN 46204-2288
317-232-8888

INDIANA
Small Business
Development Centers
Economic Development
Council
One North Capitol, Suite 420
Indianapolis, IN 46204
317-264-6871

IOWA
Iowa Economic
Development
200 E Grand
Des Moines, IA 50309
515-242-4817

IOWA
Small Business
Development Center
Iowa State University
137 Lynn Avenue
Ames, IA 50010
515-292-6351

KANSAS
Kansas Commerce
Development
700 SW Harrison #1300
Topeka, KS 66603-3712
913-296-3480

KENTUCKY
Kentucky Economic
Development
2400 Capital Plaza Tower
500 Metro St.
Frankfort, KY 40601
502-564-7670

KENTUCKY
Small Business
Development Center
University of Kentucky
225 Business &
Economics Bldg.
Lexington, KY 40506-0034
606-257-7668

LOUISIANA
Louisiana Economic
Development
P. O. Box 94185
Baton Rouge, 70804-9815
504-342-5388

LOUISIANA
Small Business
Development Center
Northeast Louisiana
University
College of Business
Administration
700 University Ave.
Monroe, LA 71209-6435
318-342-5506

MAINE
Maine Economic
Community Development
33 Stone St.
Augusta, ME 04333
207-287-2656

MAINE
Small Business
Development Center
University of
Southern Maine
96 Falmouth St.
Portland, ME 04103
207-780-4420

MARYLAND
Maryland Business
Development Office
217 E. Redwood St.
10th Floor
Baltimore, MD 21201
410-333-6985

MARYLAND
Small Business
Development Center
Dept. of Economic &
Employment Development
217 East Redwood St.
Baltimore, MD 21202
410-333-6995

MASSACHUSETTS
Mass. Economic Affairs
1 Ashburton Place, #1201
Boston, MA 02108
617-727-8380

MASSACHUSETTS
Small Business
Development Center
University of Massachusetts-
Amherst
Room 205, School of
Management
Amherst, MA 01003
413-545-6301

MICHIGAN
Michigan Department
of Commerce
116 W. Allegan
Lansing, MI 48933
517-373-1820

MICHIGAN
Small Business
Development Center
2727 Second Avenue
Detroit, MI 48201
313-964-1798

MINNESOTA
Department of Trade and
Economic Development
500 Metro Sq. Building
121 E. 7th Place
St. Paul MN 55101
612-297-1291

MISSISSIPPI
Mississippi Department of
Economic Development
P. O. Box 849
Jackson, MS 39205
601-359-3449

MISSISSIPPI
Small Business
Development Center
University of Mississippi
Old Chemistry Bldg.
Suite 216
University, MS 38677
601-232-5001

MISSOURI
Missouri Department of
Economic Development
P. O. Box 1157
Jefferson City, MO 65102
314-751-4962

MISSOURI
Small Business
Development Center
University of Missouri
300 University Place
Columbia, MO 65211
314-882-0344

MONTANA
Montana Economic
Development Board
P.O. Box 20051
Helena, MT 59620
406-444-3814

MONTANA
Small Business
Development Center
1424 9th Avenue
Helena, MT 59620
406-444-4780

NEBRASKA
Nebraska Board of
Economic Development
301 Centennial Mall S.
P. O. Box 94666
Lincoln, NE 68509
402-471-3111 or
1-800-426-6505

NEBRASKA
Business Development
Center
1313 Farnam
Omaha, NE 68182
402-595-2381

NEVADA
Nevada Economic
Development
5151 S. Carson St.
Carson City, NV 89710
702-687-4325

NEVADA
Small Business
Development Center
University of Nevada, Reno
College of Business Administration-032, Room 411
Reno, NV 89557-0100
702-784-1717

NEW HAMPSHIRE
New Hampshire Department
of Economic Development
P.O. Box 1856
Concord, NH 03302-1856
603-271-2341

NEW HAMPSHIRE
Small Business
Development Center
University of New Hampshire
108 McConnell Hall
Durham, NH 03824
603-862-2200

NEW JERSEY
NJ Economic Authority
200 S. Warren St. CN990
Trenton, NJ 08625
609-292-1800

NEW JERSEY
Small Business
Development Center
Rutgers University Graduate
School of Management
180 University Ave.
Newark, NJ 07102
201-648-5950

NEW MEXICO
New Mexico Economic
Development
1100 St. Francis Dr.
Santa Fe, NM 87503
505-827-0300

NEW MEXICO
Small Business
Development Center
Santa Fe
Community College
P.O. Box 4187
Santa Fe, NM 87502-4187
505-438-1362

NEW YORK
New York Department of
Economic Development
1 Commerce Plaza
Albany, NY 12245
518-473-1325

NEW YORK
State Small Business
Development Center
State University of
New York
SUNY Central Plaza, S-523
Albany, NY 12246
518-443-5398

NORTH CAROLINA
N. Carolina Business
and Industry
430 N. Salisbury
Raleigh, NC 27603
919-733-4151

NORTH CAROLINA
Small Business
Development Center
University of North Carolina
4509 Creedmoore Rd.,
Suite 201
Raleigh, NC 27612
919-571-4154

NORTH DAKOTA
N. Dakota Economic
Development and Finance
1833 E. Bismarck Expressway
Bismarck, ND 58504
701-328-5300

NORTH DAKOTA
Small Business
Development Center
University of North Dakota
118 Gamble Hall, UND
Box 7308
Grand Fork, ND 58202
(701) 777-3700

OHIO
Ohio Economic Development
77 S. High St.
Columbus, OH 43266
614-466-2317

OKLAHOMA
Oklahoma Department of
Commerce
P. O. Box 26980
Oklahoma City, OK
73126-0980
405-843-9770

OKLAHOMA
Small Business
Development Center
Southeastern Okla. State Univ.
P.O.; Box 2584, Station A
Durant, OK 74701
405-924-0277

OREGON
Ore. Economic Development
775 Summer NE
Salem, OR 97310
503-986-0123

OREGON
Small Business
Development Center
Lane Community College
44 W. Broadway, Suite 501
Eugene, OR 97401-3021
503-726-2250

PENNSYLVANIA
Pennsylvania Department of
Commerce
433 Forum Building
Harrisburg, PA 17120
717-787-3003

PENNSYLVANIA
Small Business
Development Center
The Wharton School
University of Pennsylvania
444 Vance Hall
3733 Spruce Street
Philadelphia, PA 19104-6374
215-898-1219

RHODE ISLAND
Rhode Island Department of
Economic Development
7 Jackson Walkway
Providence, RI 02903
401-277-2601

RHODE ISLAND
Small Business
Development Center
Bryant College
1150 Douglas Pike
Smithfield, RI 02917
401-232-6111

SOUTH CAROLINA
South Carolina Department
of Commerce
P.O. Box 927
Columbia, SC 29202
803-737-0400

SOUTH CAROLINA
Small Business
Development Center
University of
South Carolina
College of
Business Administration
Columbia, SC 29201-9980
803-777-4907

SOUTH DAKOTA
South Dakota Economic
Development
711 E Wells Ave
Pierie, SD 57501
605-773-5032

SOUTH DAKOTA
Small Business
Development Center
University of
SouthDakota
414 E. Clark
Vermillion, SD 57069
605-677-5279

TENNESSEE
Tennessee Economic
Development
320 6th Ave N.
8th Floor
Nashville, TN. 37243-0405
615-741-1888

TENNESSEE
Small Business
Development Center
Memphis State University
Bldg. 1, South Campus
Memphis, TN 38152
901-678-2500

TEXAS
Texas Department of
Commerce
P. O. Box 12728
Austin, TX 78711-2728
512-472-5059

TEXAS-DALLAS
Small Business
Development Center
1402 Corinth St.
Dallas, TX 75215
214-565-5850

TEXAS-HOUSTON
Small Business
Development Center
1100 Louisiana, Suite 500
Houston, TX 77002
713-752-8444

TEXAS-LUBBOCK
N.W. Texas Small Business
Development Center
Texas Tech University
2579 S. Loop 289
Suite 114
Lubbock, TX 79423
806-745-3973

UTAH
Utah Community of
Economic Development
324 S. State
#500
Salt Lake City, UT 84114
801-538-8700

UTAH
Small Business
Development Center
102 West 500 South
Suite 315
Salt Lake City, UT 84101
801-581-7905

VERMONT
Vermont Economic
Development
109 State St.
Montpelier, VT 05609
802-828-3221

VERMONT
Small Business
Development Center
Vermont Technical College
P.O. Box 422
Randolph, VT 05060
802-728-9101

VIRGINIA
Virginia Economic
Development
P.O. Box 798
Richmond, VA 23206-0798
804-371-8106

WASHINGTON
Washington Community, Trade
& Economic Development
906 Columbia St. SW
P.O. Box 48300
Olympia, WA 98504-8300
206-753-7426

WASHINGTON
Small Business
Development Center
Washington State University
Kruegel Hall, Ste. 135
Pullman, WA 99164-4727
509-335-1576

WEST VIRGINIA
W. Virginia Economic
Development Authority
1018 Kanawha Blvd. E.
#501
Charleston, WV-25301-2827
304-558-3650

WEST VIRGINIA
Small Business
Development Center
950 Kanawha Blvd.
Charleston, WV 25301
304-558-2960

WISCONSIN
Wisconsin Economic
Development Authority
1 S. Pinckney, St.
#500
P.O. Box 1728
Madison, WI 53701-1728
608-266-7884

WISCONSIN
Small Business
Development Center
University of Wisconsin
432 North Lake Street
Room 423
Madison, WI 53706
608-263-7794

WYOMING
Wyoming Economic
Development
Barrett Building
4th Floor N.
Cheyenne, WY 82002
307-777-7284

Venture Capitalists

VENTURE CAPITALISTS

Select three or four venture capital firms from the list and send your executive summary to them by mail. If you do not get a response in three weeks, then I would give them a call and ask them if they have any interest in your proposal. You will have to give them time to go over your information and make a decision on whether to proceed with negotiations based on the information contained in your executive summary.

HICKORY VENTURE CAPITAL CORP.

200 West Court Sq.

Huntsville, AL 35801

PHONE #: 205-539-1931

FAX #: 205-539-5130

AREA OF INVESTMENT REGION CONSIDERED: SOUTH & MIDWEST UNITED STATES

MOST DESIRED INVESTMENTS IN FIELDS OF: OPEN TO MANY INVESTMENTS, GENERAL HEALTH CARE, HIGH TECHNOLOGY, ELECTRONICS, LIFE SCIENCES, MEDICINE, ENVIRONMENTAL, BIOTECHNOLOGY, INFORMATIONAL SERVICES, SERVICE COMPANIES, MANUFACTURING, COMMUNICATIONS

POSSIBLE CONSIDERATION FOR INVESTMENT IN: SOME START-UP COMPANIES, OPEN TO OTHER PROPOSALS

NO INVESTMENT INTEREST WHATSOEVER IN: REAL ESTATE, OIL OR GAS

MINIMUM AND MAXIMUM INVESTMENT DOLLAR AMOUNT: $1,000,000 to $7,000,000

SUNDANCE VENTURE PARTNERS, L.P.

400 East Van Buren

Suite 650

Phoenix, AZ 85004

PHONE #: 602-252-5373

FAX #: 602-252-1450

AREA OF INVESTMENT REGION CONSIDERED: WEST COAST

MOST DESIRED INVESTMENTS IN FIELDS OF: OPEN TO MANY INVESTMENTS. HIGH TECHNOLOGY, COMPUTER PRODUCTS, BIOTECHNOLOGY, INFORMATIONAL SERVICES, SERVICE COMPANIES, MANUFACTURING, COMMUNICATIONS, ELECTRONICS, LIFE SCIENCES, MEDICINE, ENVIRONMENTAL

POSSIBLE CONSIDERATION FOR INVESTMENT IN: OPEN TO OTHER PROPOSALS

NO INVESTMENT INTEREST WHATSOEVER IN: REAL ESTATE, OIL OR GAS

MINIMUM AND MAXIMUM INVESTMENT DOLLAR AMOUNT: $2,000,000+

BRENTWOOD ASSOCIATES

11150 Santa Monica Blvd.

Suite 1200

LA, CA 90025

PHONE #: 310-477-6611

FAX #: 310-477-1011

AREA OF INVESTMENT REGION CONSIDERED: UNITED STATES

MOST DESIRED INVESTMENTS IN FIELDS OF: OPEN TO MANY INVESTMENTS IN MEDICAL FIELDS, MEDICAL CARE, MEDICAL PRODUCTS, BIOTECHNOLOGY, LIFE SCIENCES

POSSIBLE CONSIDERATION FOR INVESTMENT IN: SOME START-UP COMPANIES

NO INVESTMENT INTEREST WHATSOEVER IN: ALL OTHER AREAS

MINIMUM AND MAXIMUM INVESTMENT DOLLAR AMOUNT: $500,000 to $10,000,000+

ENTERPRISE PARTNERS

12011 San Vincente Blvd.

Suite 330

Los Angeles, CA 90049

PHONE #: 310-476-3000

FAX #: 310-476-3030

AREA OF INVESTMENT REGION CONSIDERED: SOUTHERN CALIFORNIA

MOST DESIRED INVESTMENTS IN FIELDS OF: INFORMATION TECHNOLOGY, HEALTH CARE PRODUCTS, COMPUTER HARDWARE AND SOFTWARE

POSSIBLE CONSIDERATION FOR INVESTMENT IN: NO OTHER FIELDS

NO INVESTMENT INTEREST WHATSOEVER IN: ALL OTHER FIELDS

MINIMUM AND MAXIMUM INVESTMENT DOLLAR AMOUNT: $1,000,000+

AVALON VENTURES

1020 Prospect Street, Suite 405

La Jolla, CA 92037

PHONE #: 619-454-3803

FAX #: 619-454-5329

AREA OF INVESTMENT REGION CONSIDERED: WESTERN UNITED STATES

MOST DESIRED INVESTMENTS IN FIELDS OF: BIOTECHNOLOGY AND BIOMEDICAL, BIOPHARMACEUTICAL COMPANIES ONLY. PREFERS START-UP COMPANIES

POSSIBLE CONSIDERATION FOR INVESTMENT IN: NO OTHER FIELDS

NO INVESTMENT INTEREST WHATSOEVER IN: ALL OTHER FIELDS

MINIMUM AND MAXIMUM INVESTMENT DOLLAR AMOUNT: VARIES

OXFORD PARTNERS

614 Lel-Medio Ave.

Pacifas Palacadis, CA 90272

PHONE #: 310-454-9812

FAX #: 310-454-9813

AREA OF INVESTMENT REGION CONSIDERED: UNITED STATES

MOST DESIRED INVESTMENTS IN FIELDS OF: MEDICAL PRODUCTS, BIOTECHNOLOGY, LIFE SCIENCES, MEDICINE, GENERAL HEALTH CARE

POSSIBLE CONSIDERATION FOR INVESTMENT IN: START-UP COMPANIES IN THESE FIELDS ONLY

NO INVESTMENT INTEREST WHATSOEVER IN: ALL OTHER FIELDS

MINIMUM AND MAXIMUM INVESTMENT DOLLAR AMOUNT: $1,000,000+

EL DORADO VENTURES

800 E. Colorado Blvd.

Suite 530

Pasadena, CA 91101

PHONE #: 818-793-1936

FAX #: 818-793-2613

AREA OF INVESTMENT REGION CONSIDERED: WESTERN UNITED STATES

MOST DESIRED INVESTMENTS IN FIELDS OF: OPEN TO MANY INVESTMENTS. HIGH TECHNOLOGY, COMPUTER PRODUCTS, BIOTECHNOLOGY, INFORMATIONAL SERVICES, SERVICE COMPANIES, MANUFACTURING, COMMUNICATIONS, ELECTRONICS, LIFE SCIENCES, MEDICINE, ENVIRONMENTAL

POSSIBLE CONSIDERATION FOR INVESTMENT IN: SOME START-UP COMPANIES, OPEN TO OTHER PROPOSALS

NO INVESTMENT INTEREST WHATSOEVER IN: MOVIES, REAL ESTATE, OIL

MINIMUM AND MAXIMUM INVESTMENT DOLLAR AMOUNT: $1,000,000+

SPECTRA ENTERPRISE ASSOC. LIMITED / NEW ENTERPRISE ASSOC.

P. O. Box 7688

Thousands Oaks, CA 91359

PHONE #: 818-865-0213

FAX #: 818-865-1309

AREA OF INVESTMENT REGION CONSIDERED: UNITED STATES

MOST DESIRED INVESTMENTS IN FIELDS OF: HIGH TECHNOLOGY, COMPUTER PRODUCTS, BIOTECHNOLOGY, INFORMATIONAL SERVICES, COMMUNICATIONS, ELECTRONICS, LIFE SCIENCES, MEDICINE, ENVIRONMENTAL

POSSIBLE CONSIDERATION FOR INVESTMENT IN: SOME START-UP COMPANIES

NO INVESTMENT INTEREST WHATSOEVER IN: ALL OTHER FIELDS

MINIMUM AND MAXIMUM INVESTMENT DOLLAR AMOUNT: $500,000+

CALSAFE CAPITAL CORP.

245 E. Main St.

Suite 107

Alhambra, CA 91801

PHONE #: 818-289-3400

FAX #: 818-300-8025

AREA OF INVESTMENT REGION CONSIDERED: CALIFORNIA

MOST DESIRED INVESTMENTS IN FIELDS OF: OPEN TO MANY INVESTMENTS. HEALTH CARE, BIOTECHNOLOGY, HIGH TECHNOLOGY, RESTAURANTS, HOTELS, MEDICAL PRODUCTS, ELECTRONICS, LIFE SCIENCES, MEDICINE, ENVIRONMENTAL

POSSIBLE CONSIDERATION FOR INVESTMENT IN: OPEN TO MANY PROPOSALS, WORKS WITH SMALL COMPANIES

NO INVESTMENT INTEREST WHATSOEVER IN: REAL ESTATE, MOVIES, OIL & GAS

MINIMUM AND MAXIMUM INVESTMENT DOLLAR AMOUNT: $50,000 to $300,000

DOMAIN ASSOCIATES

650 Town Center Drive

Suite 810

Costa Mesa, CA 92626

PHONE #: 714-434-6227

FAX #: 714-754-6802

AREA OF INVESTMENT REGION CONSIDERED: UNITED STATES

MOST DESIRED INVESTMENTS IN FIELDS OF: BIOTECHNOLOGY, HEALTH CARE, LIFE SCIENCES, MEDICINE

POSSIBLE CONSIDERATION FOR INVESTMENT IN: MAY LOOK AT START-UP COMPANIES IN THIS FIELD ONLY

NO INVESTMENT INTEREST WHATSOEVER IN: ALL OTHER FIELDS

MINIMUM AND MAXIMUM INVESTMENT DOLLAR AMOUNT: $500,000 to $2,000,000

OXFORD BIOSCIENCE PARTNERS

650 Town Center Dr.

Suite 810

Costa Mesa, CA 92626

PHONE #: 714-754-5719

FAX #: 714-754-6802

AREA OF INVESTMENT REGION CONSIDERED: UNITED STATES

MOST DESIRED INVESTMENTS IN FIELDS OF: MEDICAL PRODUCTS, BIOTECHNOLOGY, LIFE SCIENCES, MEDICINE

POSSIBLE CONSIDERATION FOR INVESTMENT IN: START-UP COMPANIES IN THESE FIELDS ONLY

NO INVESTMENT INTEREST WHATSOEVER IN: ALL OTHER FIELDS

MINIMUM AND MAXIMUM INVESTMENT DOLLAR AMOUNT: $1,000,000+

DSV PARTNERS

620 Newport Center Drive.

Suite 990

Newport Beach, CA 92660

PHONE #: 714-759-5657

FAX #: 714-760-6947

AREA OF INVESTMENT REGION CONSIDERED: UNITED STATES

MOST DESIRED INVESTMENTS IN FIELDS OF: CHEMICALS, COMPUTER SOFTWARE, BIOTECHNOLOGY, LIFE SCIENCES, MEDICINE

POSSIBLE CONSIDERATION FOR INVESTMENT IN: NO OTHER FIELDS

NO INVESTMENT INTEREST WHATSOEVER IN: ALL OTHER FIELDS

MINIMUM AND MAXIMUM INVESTMENT DOLLAR AMOUNT: $1,000,000 to $5,000,000

BRENTWOOD ASSOCIATES

1920 Main St.

Suite 820

Irvine, CA 92714

PHONE #: 714-251-1010

FAX #: 714-251-1011

AREA OF INVESTMENT REGION CONSIDERED: UNITED STATES

MOST DESIRED INVESTMENTS IN FIELDS OF: MEDICAL CARE, MEDICAL PRODUCTS, ELECTRONICS, LIFE SCIENCES, MEDICINE

POSSIBLE CONSIDERATION FOR INVESTMENT IN: SOME START-UP COMPANIES

NO INVESTMENT INTEREST WHATSOEVER IN: ALL OTHER AREAS

MINIMUM AND MAXIMUM INVESTMENT DOLLAR AMOUNT: $500,000 to $10,000,000+

CROSSPOINT VENTURE PARTNERS

One First St.

Los Altos, CA 94022

PHONE #: 415-948-8300

FAX #: 415-948-6172

AREA OF INVESTMENT REGION CONSIDERED: UNITED STATES

MOST DESIRED INVESTMENTS IN FIELDS OF: OPEN TO MANY INVESTMENTS. HIGH TECHNOLOGY, COMPUTER PRODUCTS, BIOTECHNOLOGY, INFORMATIONAL SERVICES, ELECTRONICS, LIFE SCIENCES, MEDICINE, ENVIRONMENTAL, SERVICE COMPANIES, MANUFACTURING, COMMUNICATIONS

POSSIBLE CONSIDERATION FOR INVESTMENT IN: SOME START-UP COMPANIES, OPEN TO OTHER PROPOSALS

NO INVESTMENT INTEREST WHATSOEVER IN: REAL ESTATE, OIL OR GAS

MINIMUM AND MAXIMUM INVESTMENT DOLLAR AMOUNT: $250,000+

CROSSPOINT VENTURE PARTNERS

18552 MacArthur Blvd.

Suite 400

Irvine, CA 94022

PHONE #: 714-852-1611

FAX #: 714-852-9804

AREA OF INVESTMENT REGION CONSIDERED: UNITED STATES

MOST DESIRED INVESTMENTS IN FIELDS OF: OPEN TO MANY INVESTMENTS. HIGH TECHNOLOGY, COMPUTER PRODUCTS, BIOTECHNOLOGY, INFORMATIONAL SERVICES, ELECTRONICS, LIFE SCIENCES, MEDICINE, ENVIRONMENTAL, SERVICE COMPANIES, MANUFACTURING, COMMUNICATIONS

POSSIBLE CONSIDERATION FOR INVESTMENT IN: SOME START-UP COMPANIES, OPEN TO OTHER PROPOSALS

NO INVESTMENT INTEREST WHATSOEVER IN: REAL ESTATE, OIL OR GAS

MINIMUM AND MAXIMUM INVESTMENT DOLLAR AMOUNT: $250,000+

NIPPON ENTERPRISE DEVELOPMENT CORP.

3000 Sand Hill Rd.

Building 4, Suite 235

Menlo Park, CA 94025

PHONE #: 415-854-8760

FAX #: 415-854-8083

AREA OF INVESTMENT REGION CONSIDERED: UNITED STATES

MOST DESIRED INVESTMENTS IN FIELDS OF: HIGH TECHNOLOGY, COMPUTER PRODUCTS, BIOTECHNOLOGY, INFORMATIONAL SERVICES, ELECTRONICS, LIFE SCIENCES, MEDICINE, ENVIRONMENTAL

POSSIBLE CONSIDERATION FOR INVESTMENT IN: NO OTHER FIELDS

NO INVESTMENT INTEREST WHATSOEVER IN: ALL OTHER FIELDS

MINIMUM AND MAXIMUM INVESTMENT DOLLAR AMOUNT: $5,000,000+

NORTHWEST VENTURE CAPITAL

3000 Sand Hill Rd.

Building 3, Suite 105

Menlo Park, CA 94025

PHONE #: 415-854-6366

FAX #: 415-854-6652

AREA OF INVESTMENT REGION CONSIDERED: UNITED STATES

MOST DESIRED INVESTMENTS IN FIELDS OF: OPEN TO MANY INVESTMENTS. HIGH TECHNOLOGY, COMPUTER PRODUCTS, BIOTECHNOLOGY, INFORMATIONAL SERVICES, ELECTRONICS, LIFE SCIENCES, MEDICINE, ENVIRONMENTAL, SERVICE COMPANIES, MANUFACTURING, COMMUNICATIONS

POSSIBLE CONSIDERATION FOR INVESTMENT IN: SOME START-UP COMPANIES

NO INVESTMENT INTEREST WHATSOEVER IN: REAL ESTATE, OIL OR GAS

MINIMUM AND MAXIMUM INVESTMENT DOLLAR AMOUNT: $1,500,000 to $5,000,000

DELPHI BIOVENTURES, L.P.

3000 Sand Hill Rd.

Building 1, Suite 135

Menlo Park, CA 94025

PHONE #: 415-854-9650

FAX #: 415-854-2961

AREA OF INVESTMENT REGION CONSIDERED: UNITED STATES

MOST DESIRED INVESTMENTS IN FIELDS OF: BIOTECHNOLOGY, HEALTH CARE, HEALTH CARE PRODUCTS, COMPUTER SOFTWARE FOR MEDICAL, LIFE SCIENCES, MEDICINE

POSSIBLE CONSIDERATION FOR INVESTMENT IN: NO OTHER FIELDS

NO INVESTMENT INTEREST WHATSOEVER IN: ALL OTHER FIELDS

MINIMUM AND MAXIMUM INVESTMENT DOLLAR AMOUNT: $1,000,000 to $2,000,000

MATRIX PARTNERS

2500 Sand Hill Rd.

Suite 113

Menlo Park, CA 94025

PHONE #: 415-854-3131

FAX #: 415-854-3296

AREA OF INVESTMENT REGION CONSIDERED: UNITED STATES

MOST DESIRED INVESTMENTS IN FIELDS OF: HIGH TECHNOLOGY, COMMUNICATIONS, COMPUTER SOFTWARE, ELECTRONICS, LIFE SCIENCES

POSSIBLE CONSIDERATION FOR INVESTMENT IN: START-UP COMPANIES IN THESE FIELDS ONLY

NO INVESTMENT INTEREST WHATSOEVER IN: ALL OTHER FIELDS

MINIMUM AND MAXIMUM INVESTMENT DOLLAR AMOUNT: $1,000,000+

BRENTWOOD ASSOCIATES

2730 Sand Hill Rd.

Suite 250

Menlo Park, CA 94025

PHONE #: 415-854-7691

FAX #: 415-854-9513

AREA OF INVESTMENT REGION CONSIDERED: UNITED STATES

MOST DESIRED INVESTMENTS IN FIELDS OF: MEDICAL CARE, MEDICAL PRODUCTS, ELECTRONICS, LIFE SCIENCES, MEDICINE

POSSIBLE CONSIDERATION FOR INVESTMENT IN: SOME START-UP COMPANIES

NO INVESTMENT INTEREST WHATSOEVER IN: ALL OTHER FIELDS

MINIMUM AND MAXIMUM INVESTMENT DOLLAR AMOUNT: $500,000 to $10,000,000+

MCCOWN DE LEEUW & CO.

3000 Sand Hill Road.

Bldg. 3, Suite 290

Menlo Park, CA 94025

PHONE #: 415-854-6000

FAX #: 415-854-0853

AREA OF INVESTMENT REGION CONSIDERED: UNITED STATES

MOST DESIRED INVESTMENTS IN FIELDS OF: OPEN TO MANY INVESTMENTS. HIGH TECHNOLOGY, COMPUTER PRODUCTS, BIOTECHNOLOGY, INFORMATIONAL SERVICES, ELECTRONICS, LIFE SCIENCES, MEDICINE, ENVIRONMENTAL, SERVICE COMPANIES, MANUFACTURING, COMMUNICATIONS

POSSIBLE CONSIDERATION FOR INVESTMENT IN: OPEN TO OTHER PROPOSALS

NO INVESTMENT INTEREST WHATSOEVER IN: REAL ESTATE, OIL OR GAS

MINIMUM AND MAXIMUM INVESTMENT DOLLAR AMOUNT: MINIMUM AMOUNT GREATER THAN $20,000,000+

MENLO VENTURES

3000 Sand Hill Rd.

Building 4, Suite 100

Menlo Park, CA 94025

PHONE #: 415-854-8540

FAX #: 415-854-7059

AREA OF INVESTMENT REGION CONSIDERED: WEST COAST

MOST DESIRED INVESTMENTS IN FIELDS OF: COMPUTER HARDWARE, COMPUTER SOFTWARE, MEDICAL, COMMUNICATIONS, ELECTRONICS, LIFE SCIENCES, MEDICINE

POSSIBLE CONSIDERATION FOR INVESTMENT IN: SOME START-UP COMPANIES IN THESE FIELDS ONLY

NO INVESTMENT INTEREST WHATSOEVER IN: ALL OTHER FIELDS

MINIMUM AND MAXIMUM INVESTMENT DOLLAR AMOUNT: $250,000+

NEW ENTERPRISE ASSOC.

3000 Sand Hill Rd.

Suite 235 Building 4

Menlo Park, CA 94025

PHONE #: 415-854-2660

FAX #: 415-854-8083

AREA OF INVESTMENT REGION CONSIDERED: UNITED STATES

MOST DESIRED INVESTMENTS IN FIELDS OF: HIGH TECHNOLOGY, COMPUTER PRODUCTS, BIOTECHNOLOGY, INFORMATIONAL SERVICES, COMMUNICATIONS, ELECTRONICS, LIFE SCIENCES, MEDICINE, ENVIRONMENTAL

POSSIBLE CONSIDERATION FOR INVESTMENT IN: SOME START-UP COMPANIES

NO INVESTMENT INTEREST WHATSOEVER IN: ALL OTHER FIELDS

MINIMUM AND MAXIMUM INVESTMENT DOLLAR AMOUNT: $500,000+

MEDICUS VENTURE PARTNERS

2180 Sand Hill Rd.

Suite 400

Menlo Park, CA 94025

PHONE #: 415-854-7100

FAX #: 415-854-5700

AREA OF INVESTMENT REGION CONSIDERED: WEST COAST

MOST DESIRED INVESTMENTS IN FIELDS OF: MEDICAL PRODUCTS ONLY

POSSIBLE CONSIDERATION FOR INVESTMENT IN: START-UP COMPANIES IN THIS FIELD ONLY

NO INVESTMENT INTEREST WHATSOEVER IN: ALL OTHER FIELDS

MINIMUM AND MAXIMUM INVESTMENT DOLLAR AMOUNT: $100,000, CASE BY CASE

MERRILY, PICKARD, ANDERSON & EYRE

2480 Sand Hill Rd.

Suite 200

Menlo Park, CA 94025

PHONE #: 415-854-8600

FAX #: 415-854-0345

AREA OF INVESTMENT REGION CONSIDERED: UNITED STATES

MOST DESIRED INVESTMENTS IN FIELDS OF: HIGH TECHNOLOGY, COMPUTER HARDWARE AND SOFTWARE, INFORMATIONAL SERVICES, COMMUNICATIONS, ELECTRONICS

POSSIBLE CONSIDERATION FOR INVESTMENT IN: SOME START-UP COMPANIES IN THESE FIELDS ONLY

NO INVESTMENT INTEREST WHATSOEVER IN: ALL OTHER FIELDS

MINIMUM AND MAXIMUM INVESTMENT DOLLAR AMOUNT: $1,000,000+

INSTITUTIONAL VENTURE PARTNERS

3000 Sand Hill Rd.

Building 2, Suite 290

Menlo Park, CA 94025

PHONE #: 415-854-0132

FAX #: 415-854-5762

AREA OF INVESTMENT REGION CONSIDERED: WEST COAST

MOST DESIRED INVESTMENTS IN FIELDS OF: BIOTECHNOLOGY, COMPUTER HARDWARE, COMPUTER SOFTWARE, DATA COMMUNICATIONS, ELECTRONICS, LIFE SCIENCES, MEDICINE, ENVIRONMENTAL, TELECOMMUNICATIONS

POSSIBLE CONSIDERATION FOR INVESTMENT IN: START-UP COMPANIES

NO INVESTMENT INTEREST WHATSOEVER IN: ALL OTHER FIELDS

MINIMUM AND MAXIMUM INVESTMENT DOLLAR AMOUNT: $1,000,000 to $3,000,000

CANAAN PARTNERS

2884 Sand Hill Rd.

Bldg. 1, Suite 115.

Menlo Park, CA 94025

PHONE #: 415-854-8092

FAX #: 415-854-8127

AREA OF INVESTMENT REGION CONSIDERED: UNITED STATES

MOST DESIRED INVESTMENTS IN FIELDS OF: OPEN TO MANY INVESTMENTS IN MEDICAL AND HEALTH CARE FIELDS, BIOTECHNOLOGY, LIFE SCIENCES, MEDICINE, SERVICE COMPANIES, FINANCIAL SERVICE COMPANIES, DISTRIBUTION COMPANIES.

POSSIBLE CONSIDERATION FOR INVESTMENT IN: SOME EARLY STAGE COMPANIES IN THESE FIELDS ONLY

NO INVESTMENT INTEREST WHATSOEVER IN: ALL OTHER FIELDS

MINIMUM AND MAXIMUM INVESTMENT DOLLAR AMOUNT: $2,500,000 to $15,000,000

OAK INVESTMENT PARTNERS

3000 Sand Hill Rd.

Building 3, Suite 240

Menlo Park, CA 94025

PHONE #: 415-854-8825

FAX #: 415-854-5259

AREA OF INVESTMENT REGION CONSIDERED: UNITED STATES

MOST DESIRED INVESTMENTS IN FIELDS OF: MEDICAL PRODUCTS, SPECIALITY RETAILING, LIFE SCIENCES, MEDICINE, GENERAL HEALTH CARE

POSSIBLE CONSIDERATION FOR INVESTMENT IN: NO OTHER FIELDS

NO INVESTMENT INTEREST WHATSOEVER IN: ALL OTHER FIELDS

MINIMUM AND MAXIMUM INVESTMENT DOLLAR AMOUNT: $2,000,000+

COMDISCO VENTURE GROUP

3000 Sand Hill Rd.

Building 2, Suite 210

Menlo Park, CA 94025

PHONE #: 415-854-9484

FAX #: 415-854-4026

AREA OF INVESTMENT REGION CONSIDERED: UNITED STATES

MOST DESIRED INVESTMENTS IN FIELDS OF: OPEN TO MANY INVESTMENTS. HIGH TECHNOLOGY, COMPUTER PRODUCTS, BIOTECHNOLOGY, INFORMATIONAL SERVICES, ELECTRONICS, LIFE SCIENCES, MEDICINE, ENVIRONMENTAL, SERVICE COMPANIES, MANUFACTURING, COMMUNICATIONS

POSSIBLE CONSIDERATION FOR INVESTMENT IN: SOME START-UP COMPANIES, THEY WILL DO DEBT FINANCING

NO INVESTMENT INTEREST WHATSOEVER IN: REAL ESTATE, OIL OR GAS

MINIMUM AND MAXIMUM INVESTMENT DOLLAR AMOUNT: $250,000 + VARIES

NEW ENTERPRISE ASSOC.

Russ Building

235 Montgomery St.

San Francisco, CA 94104

PHONE #: 415-956-1579

FAX #: 415-981-4168

AREA OF INVESTMENT REGION CONSIDERED: UNITED STATES

MOST DESIRED INVESTMENTS IN FIELDS OF: HIGH TECHNOLOGY, COMPUTER PRODUCTS, BIOTECHNOLOGY, ELECTRONICS, LIFE SCIENCES, MEDICINE, ENVIRONMENTAL, INFORMATIONAL SERVICES, COMMUNICATIONS

POSSIBLE CONSIDERATION FOR INVESTMENT IN: SOME START-UP COMPANIES

NO INVESTMENT INTEREST WHATSOEVER IN: ALL OTHER FIELDS

MINIMUM AND MAXIMUM INVESTMENT DOLLAR AMOUNT: $500,000+

HAMBRECHT & QUIST INC

One Bush St.

18th Floor

San Francisco, CA 94104

PHONE #: 415-576-3300

FAX #: 415-576-3621

AREA OF INVESTMENT REGION CONSIDERED: UNITED STATES

MOST DESIRED INVESTMENTS IN FIELDS OF: MEDICAL PRODUCTS, COMPUTER HARDWARE & SOFTWARE, CONSUMER PRODUCTS, ELECTRONICS, LIFE SCIENCES, ENVIRONMENTAL, MANUFACTURING

POSSIBLE CONSIDERATION FOR INVESTMENT IN: OPEN TO OTHER INVESTMENTS

NO INVESTMENT INTEREST WHATSOEVER IN: NO START-UP COMPANIES, REAL ESTATE, OIL AND GAS

MINIMUM AND MAXIMUM INVESTMENT DOLLAR AMOUNT: $1,000,000+

WEISS, PECK & GREER VENTURE PARTNERS, L.P.

555 California St.
Suite 4760
San Francisco, CA 94104
PHONE #: 415-622-6864
FAX #: 415-989-5108

AREA OF INVESTMENT REGION CONSIDERED: UNITED STATES

MOST DESIRED INVESTMENTS IN FIELDS OF: HIGH TECHNOLOGY PRODUCTS AND FIELDS, ONLY

POSSIBLE CONSIDERATION FOR INVESTMENT IN: NO OTHER FIELDS

NO INVESTMENT INTEREST WHATSOEVER IN: ALL OTHER FIELDS

MINIMUM AND MAXIMUM INVESTMENT DOLLAR AMOUNT: $5,000,000+

ENDEAVOR CAPITAL MANAGEMENT

1880 Pacific Ave.

Suite 703

San Francisco, CA 94109

PHONE #: 415-441-8986

FAX #: 415-442-4264

AREA OF INVESTMENT REGION CONSIDERED: UNITED STATES

MOST DESIRED INVESTMENTS IN FIELDS OF: INFORMATION SERVICES, NEW TECHNOLOGY, HIGH TECHNOLOGY, HEALTH CARE, ELECTRONICS, LIFE SCIENCES, MEDICAL PRODUCTS, COMPUTER SOFTWARE

POSSIBLE CONSIDERATION FOR INVESTMENT IN: WILL LOOK AT EARLY STAGE COMPANIES IN THESE FIELDS ONLY

NO INVESTMENT INTEREST WHATSOEVER IN: ALL OTHER FIELDS

MINIMUM AND MAXIMUM INVESTMENT DOLLAR AMOUNT: $500,000 to $1,500,000

ACCEL PARTNERS

One Embarcadero Center
San Francisco, CA 94111
PHONE #: 415-989-5656
FAX #: 415-989-5554

AREA OF INVESTMENT REGION CONSIDERED: UNITED STATES

MOST DESIRED INVESTMENTS IN FIELDS OF: HIGH TECHNOLOGY, HEALTH CARE, COMPUTER SOFTWARE, TELECOMMUNICATIONS, HEALTH CARE PRODUCTS, ELECTRONICS, LIFE SCIENCES, MEDICINE, ENVIRONMENTAL

POSSIBLE CONSIDERATION FOR INVESTMENT IN: NO OTHER FIELDS

NO INVESTMENT INTEREST WHATSOEVER IN: ALL OTHER FIELDS

MINIMUM AND MAXIMUM INVESTMENT DOLLAR AMOUNT: $500,000 to $6,000,000

ENTERPRISE PARTNERS

5000 Birth Street

Suite 6200

Newport Beach, CA 92660

PHONE #: 714-833-3650

FAX #:

AREA OF INVESTMENT REGION CONSIDERED: SOUTHERN CALIFORNIA

MOST DESIRED INVESTMENTS IN FIELDS OF: INFORMATION TECHNOLOGY, HEALTH CARE PRODUCTS, COMPUTER HARD-WARE AND SOFTWARE

POSSIBLE CONSIDERATION FOR INVESTMENT IN: NO OTHER FIELDS

NO INVESTMENT INTEREST WHATSOEVER IN: ALL OTHER FIELDS

MINIMUM AND MAXIMUM INVESTMENT DOLLAR AMOUNT: $1,000,000+

SUMMIT PARTNERS

499 Hamilton Ave.

Suite 200

Palo Alto, CA 94301

PHONE #: 415-321-1166

FAX #: 415-321-1188

AREA OF INVESTMENT REGION CONSIDERED: UNITED STATES

MOST DESIRED INVESTMENTS IN FIELDS OF: OPEN TO MANY INVESTMENTS. HIGH TECHNOLOGY, COMPUTER PRODUCTS, BIOTECHNOLOGY, INFORMATIONAL SERVICES, ELECTRONICS, LIFE SCIENCES, MEDICINE, ENVIRONMENTAL, SERVICE COMPANIES, MANUFACTURING, COMMUNICATIONS

POSSIBLE CONSIDERATION FOR INVESTMENT IN: OPEN TO OTHER PROPOSALS

NO INVESTMENT INTEREST WHATSOEVER IN: REAL ESTATE OIL & GAS

MINIMUM AND MAXIMUM INVESTMENT DOLLAR AMOUNT: $2,000,000 to $20,000,000

CHARTER VENTURE CAPITAL

525 University Ave.

Suite 1500

Palo Alto, CA 94301

PHONE #: 415-325-6953

FAX #: 415-325-4762

AREA OF INVESTMENT REGION CONSIDERED: UNITED STATES

MOST DESIRED INVESTMENTS IN FIELDS OF: BIOTECHNOLOGY, MEDICAL TECHNOLOGY PRODUCTS, LIFE SCIENCES, MEDICINE

POSSIBLE CONSIDERATION FOR INVESTMENT IN: START-UP COMPANIES IN THESE FIELDS ONLY

NO INVESTMENT INTEREST WHATSOEVER IN: ALL OTHER FIELDS

MINIMUM AND MAXIMUM INVESTMENT DOLLAR AMOUNT: $1,000,000+

ON SET-VENTURES /NEW ENTERPRISE ASSOC.

301 University Ave.
Palo Alto, CA 94301

PHONE #: 415-327-5470

FAX #: 415-327-5488

AREA OF INVESTMENT REGION CONSIDERED: UNITED STATES

MOST DESIRED INVESTMENTS IN FIELDS OF: HIGH TECHNOLOGY, COMPUTER PRODUCTS, BIOTECHNOLOGY, INFORMATIONAL SERVICES, ELECTRONICS, LIFE SCIENCES, MEDICINE, ENVIRONMENTAL, COMMUNICATIONS

POSSIBLE CONSIDERATION FOR INVESTMENT IN: SOME START-UP COMPANIES

NO INVESTMENT INTEREST WHATSOEVER IN: ALL OTHER FIELDS

MINIMUM AND MAXIMUM INVESTMENT DOLLAR AMOUNT: $500,000+

ASSET MANAGEMENT COMPANY

2275 East Bayshore Road.

Suite 150

Palo Alto, CA 94303

PHONE #: 415-494-7400

FAX #: 415-856-1826

AREA OF INVESTMENT REGION CONSIDERED: CALIFORNIA

MOST DESIRED INVESTMENTS IN FIELDS OF: HIGH TECHNOLOGY, BIOTECHNOLOGY, LASERS, COMPUTER HARDWARE AND SOFTWARE, MEDICAL PRODUCTS, ELECTRONICS, LIFE SCIENCES, ENVIRONMENTAL

POSSIBLE CONSIDERATION FOR INVESTMENT IN: START-UP COMPANIES IN THESE FIELDS ONLY

NO INVESTMENT INTEREST WHATSOEVER IN: ALL OTHER FIELDS

MINIMUM AND MAXIMUM INVESTMENT DOLLAR AMOUNT: $100,000 to $1,000,000

ROSEWOOD CAPITAL LP

1 Maritane Plaza, Suite 1330

San Francisco, CA 94111

PHONE #: 415-362-5526

FAX #: 415-362-1192

AREA OF INVESTMENT REGION CONSIDERED: UNITED STATES

MOST DESIRED INVESTMENTS IN FIELDS OF: ESTABLISHED COMPANIES ONLY. SERVICE INDUSTRY, CONSUMER COMPANIES, EDUCATION COMPANIES, MULTI-MEDIA, TELE-COMMUNICATIONS, SPECIALTY RETAILING

POSSIBLE CONSIDERATION FOR INVESTMENT IN: OPEN TO OTHER ESTAB-LISHED COMPANIES

NO INVESTMENT INTEREST WHATSOEVER IN: BIOTECHNOLOGY, OR START-UP COMPANIES

MINIMUM AND MAXIMUM INVESTMENT DOLLAR AMOUNT: $2,000,000 TO $10,000,000

VENROCK ASSOCIATES

755 Page Mill Rd.

Suite A 230

Palo Alto, CA 94304

PHONE #: 415-493-5577

FAX #: 415-493-6443

AREA OF INVESTMENT REGION CONSIDERED: UNITED STATES

MOST DESIRED INVESTMENTS IN FIELDS OF: LEADING EDGE TECHNOLOGY ONLY. HIGH TECHNOLOGY, BIOTECHNOLOGY, ROBOTICS, ELECTRONICS, LIFE SCIENCES, MEDICINE, ENVIRONMENTAL

POSSIBLE CONSIDERATION FOR INVESTMENT IN: NO OTHER FIELDS

NO INVESTMENT INTEREST WHATSOEVER IN: ALL OTHER FIELDS

MINIMUM AND MAXIMUM INVESTMENT DOLLAR AMOUNT: $500,000 to $2,000,000

GREYLOCK MANAGEMENT CORP

755 Page Mill Rd.

Suite B-140

Palo Alto, CA 94304

PHONE #: 415-493-5525

FAX #: 415-493-5575

AREA OF INVESTMENT REGION CONSIDERED: UNITED STATES

MOST DESIRED INVESTMENTS IN FIELDS OF: OPEN TO MANY INVESTMENTS. HIGH TECHNOLOGY, BIOTECHNOLOGY, MEDICAL PRODUCTS, MEDICAL HEALTH CARE, COMPUTER HARDWARE AND SOFTWARE, ELECTRONICS, LIFE SCIENCES, MEDICINE, ENVIRONMENTAL

POSSIBLE CONSIDERATION FOR INVESTMENT IN: SOME START-UP COMPANIES

NO INVESTMENT INTEREST WHATSOEVER IN: REAL ESTATE, OIL, GAS

MINIMUM AND MAXIMUM INVESTMENT DOLLAR AMOUNT: $1,000,000+

VAN GUARD VENTURE PARTNERS

525 University Avenue, Suite 600

Palo Alto, CA 94301

PHONE #: 415-321-2900

FAX #: 415-321-2902

AREA OF INVESTMENT REGION CONSIDERED: UNITED STATES

MOST DESIRED INVESTMENTS IN FIELDS OF: BIOTECHNOLOGY, COMPUTER HARDWARE AND SOFTWARE, COMMUNICATIONS, TELECOMMUNICATIONS

POSSIBLE CONSIDERATION FOR INVESTMENT IN: NO OTHER COMPANIES

NO INVESTMENT INTEREST WHATSOEVER IN: ALL OTHER FIELDS

MINIMUM AND MAXIMUM INVESTMENT DOLLAR AMOUNT: $500,000+

ADVENT INTERNATIONAL CORP.

2180 Sand Hill Rd.

Suite 420

Menlo Park, CA 94025

PHONE #: 415-233-7500

FAX #: 415-233-7515

AREA OF INVESTMENT REGION CONSIDERED: UNITED STATES

MOST DESIRED INVESTMENTS IN FIELDS OF: BIOTECHNOLOGY, MEDICAL PRODUCTS, COMPUTER SOFTWARE, INFORMATIONAL SERVICES, TELECOMMUNICATIONS, HIGH TECHNOLOGY, ELECTRONICS, LIFE SCIENCES, MEDICINE, ENVIRONMENTAL

POSSIBLE CONSIDERATION FOR INVESTMENT IN: INDUSTRIAL PRODUCTS, CHEMICALS, ENVIRONMENTAL, SOME START-UP COMPANIES, OPEN TO OTHER PROPOSALS.

NO INVESTMENT INTEREST WHATSOEVER IN: REAL ESTATE, OIL OR GAS.

MINIMUM AND MAXIMUM INVESTMENT DOLLAR AMOUNT: $5,000,000 to $15,000,000.

TECHNOLOGY PARTNERS

1550 Tiburon Blvd.

Suite A.

Belvedere, CA 94920

PHONE #: 415-435-1935

FAX #: 415-435-5921

AREA OF INVESTMENT REGION CONSIDERED: WEST COAST

MOST DESIRED INVESTMENTS IN FIELDS OF: MULTIMEDIA, HIGH TECHNOLOGY, MEDICAL PRODUCTS AND HEALTH CARE, ELECTRONICS, LIFE SCIENCES, MEDICINE, ENVIRONMENTAL

POSSIBLE CONSIDERATION FOR INVESTMENT IN: NO OTHER FIELDS

NO INVESTMENT INTEREST WHATSOEVER IN: ALL OTHER FIELDS

MINIMUM AND MAXIMUM INVESTMENT DOLLAR AMOUNT: $1,000,000+

GRACE VENTURES CORP.

20300 Stevens Creek Blvd.

Suite 330

Cupertino, CA 95014

PHONE #: 408-725-0774

FAX #: 408-725-0327

AREA OF INVESTMENT REGION CONSIDERED: UNITED STATES

MOST DESIRED INVESTMENTS IN FIELDS OF: COMPUTER PRODUCTS, COMPUTER SOFTWARE, MEDICAL PRODUCTS, ELECTRONICS, LIFE SCIENCES, SPECIALTY RETAIL, HEALTH SERVICES, RESTAURANTS, BIOTECHNOLOGY, COMMUNICATIONS

POSSIBLE CONSIDERATION FOR INVESTMENT IN: ESTABLISHED CONSUMER PRODUCT COMPANIES

NO INVESTMENT INTEREST WHATSOEVER IN: ALL OTHER FIELDS

MINIMUM AND MAXIMUM INVESTMENT DOLLAR AMOUNT: $1,000,000 to $3,000,000

SUNDANCE VENTURE PARTNERS, L.P.

10600 N. DeAnza Blvd.

Suite 215

Cupertino, CA 95014

PHONE #: 408-257-8100

FAX #: 408-257-8111

AREA OF INVESTMENT REGION CONSIDERED: WEST COAST

MOST DESIRED INVESTMENTS IN FIELDS OF: OPEN TO MANY INVESTMENTS. HIGH TECHNOLOGY, COMPUTER PRODUCTS, BIOTECHNOLOGY, INFORMATIONAL SERVICES, ELECTRONICS, LIFE SCIENCES, MEDICINE, ENVIRONMENTAL, SERVICE COMPANIES, MANUFACTURING, COMMUNICATIONS

POSSIBLE CONSIDERATION FOR INVESTMENT IN: OPEN TO OTHER PROPOSALS

NO INVESTMENT INTEREST WHATSOEVER IN: REAL ESTATE, OIL OR GAS

MINIMUM AND MAXIMUM INVESTMENT DOLLAR AMOUNT: $2,000,000+

EL DORADO VENTURES

20300 Stevens Creek Blvd.
Suite 395
Cupertino, CA 95014
PHONE #: 408-725-2474
FAX #: 408-252-2762

AREA OF INVESTMENT REGION CONSIDERED: WESTERN UNITED STATES

MOST DESIRED INVESTMENTS IN FIELDS OF: OPEN TO MANY INVESTMENTS. HIGH TECHNOLOGY, COMPUTER PRODUCTS, BIOTECHNOLOGY, INFORMATIONAL SERVICES, SERVICE COMPANIES, MANUFACTURING, COMMUNICATIONS, ELECTRONICS, LIFE SCIENCES, MEDICINE, ENVIRONMENTAL

POSSIBLE CONSIDERATION FOR INVESTMENT IN: SOME START-UP COMPANIES, OPEN TO OTHER PROPOSALS

NO INVESTMENT INTEREST WHATSOEVER IN: MOVIES, REAL ESTATE, OIL, GAS

MINIMUM AND MAXIMUM INVESTMENT DOLLAR AMOUNT: $1,000,000+

THE VERTICAL GROUP

338 Village LN.

Los Gatos, CA 95030

PHONE #: 408-399-4533

FAX #: 408-399-4531

AREA OF INVESTMENT REGION CONSIDERED: UNITED STATES

MOST DESIRED INVESTMENTS IN FIELDS OF: MEDICAL HEALTH CARE, MEDICAL PRODUCTS, BIOTECHNOLOGY, LIFE SCIENCES, MEDICINE

POSSIBLE CONSIDERATION FOR INVESTMENT IN: SOME START-UP COMPANIES IN THESE FIELDS ONLY

NO INVESTMENT INTEREST WHATSOEVER IN: ALL OTHER FIELDS

MINIMUM AND MAXIMUM INVESTMENT DOLLAR AMOUNT: $500,000+

KOBE STEEL USA, INC.

1735 Technology Drive

Suite 820

San Jose, CA 95110

PHONE #: 408-436-9714

FAX #: 408-436-0548

AREA OF INVESTMENT REGION CONSIDERED: UNITED STATES

MOST DESIRED INVESTMENTS IN FIELDS OF: AUTOMATION PRODUCTS, ELECTRONICS, HIGH TECHNOLOGY, COMPUTER HARDWARE, SEMI-CONDUCTORS

POSSIBLE CONSIDERATION FOR INVESTMENT IN: NO OTHER FIELDS

NO INVESTMENT INTEREST WHATSOEVER IN: ALL OTHER FIELDS

MINIMUM AND MAXIMUM INVESTMENT DOLLAR AMOUNT: $1,000,000+

ADVANCED TECHNOLOGY VENTURES

1000 El Camino Real

Suite 360

Menlo Park, CA 94025-4327

PHONE #: 415-321-8601

FAX #: 415-321-0934

AREA OF INVESTMENT REGION CONSIDERED: UNITED STATES

MOST DESIRED INVESTMENTS IN FIELDS OF: HIGH TECHNOLOGY, BIOTECHNOLOGY, HIGH PRIORITY TECHNOLOGY, ELECTRONICS, LIFE SCIENCES, MEDICINE, ENVIRONMENTAL

POSSIBLE CONSIDERATION FOR INVESTMENT IN: START-UP COMPANIES IN THESE FIELDS ONLY

NO INVESTMENT INTEREST WHATSOEVER IN: ALL OTHER FIELDS

MINIMUM AND MAXIMUM INVESTMENT DOLLAR AMOUNT: $500,000 to $2,000,000

WESTON PRESIDIO CAPITAL

343 Sansome St.

Suite 1210

San Francisco, CA 94104-1316

PHONE #: 415-398-0770

FAX #: 415-398-0990

AREA OF INVESTMENT REGION CONSIDERED: UNITED STATES

MOST DESIRED INVESTMENTS IN FIELDS OF: HIGH TECHNOLOGY, BIOTECHNOLOGY, MEDICAL PRODUCTS, HEALTH CARE, LIFE SCIENCES, MEDICINE

POSSIBLE CONSIDERATION FOR INVESTMENT IN: NO OTHER FIELDS

NO INVESTMENT INTEREST WHATSOEVER IN: ALL OTHER FIELDS

MINIMUM AND MAXIMUM INVESTMENT DOLLAR AMOUNT: $1,000,000+

TECHNOLOGY FUNDING

2000 Alameda De Las Pulgas

San Mateo, CA 94403

PHONE #: 415-345-2200

FAX #: 415-341-1400

AREA OF INVESTMENT REGION CONSIDERED: UNITED STATES

MOST DESIRED INVESTMENTS IN FIELDS OF: LIKES ESTABLISHED COMPANIES, INFORMATION TECHNOLOGIES, LIFE SCIENCES, ENVIRONMENTAL, INDUSTRIAL PRODUCTS

POSSIBLE CONSIDERATION FOR INVESTMENT IN: SOME START-UP COMPANIES IN THESE FIELDS ONLY

NO INVESTMENT INTEREST WHATSOEVER IN: ALL OTHER FIELDS

MINIMUM AND MAXIMUM INVESTMENT DOLLAR AMOUNT: $500,000 to $1,000,000

COLUMBINE VENTURE FUND LTD

6312 S. Fiddlers Green Cr. 260N

Englewood, CO 80111

PHONE #: 303-694-3222

FAX #: 303-694-9007

AREA OF INVESTMENT REGION CONSIDERED: ROCKY MOUNTAIN, TEXAS REGION

MOST DESIRED INVESTMENTS IN FIELDS OF: BIOTECHNOLOGY, HIGH TECHNOLOGY, ADVANCED MEDICAL PRODUCTS, HEALTH CARE PRODUCTS, ELECTRONICS, LIFE SCIENCES, MEDICINE

POSSIBLE CONSIDERATION FOR INVESTMENT IN: SOME START-UP COMPANIES IN THESE FIELDS ONLY

NO INVESTMENT INTEREST WHATSOEVER IN: ALL OTHER FIELDS

MINIMUM AND MAXIMUM INVESTMENT DOLLAR AMOUNT: $500,000+

THE CENTENNIAL FUNDS

1999 Broadway

Suite 2100

Denver, CO 80202

PHONE #: 303-298-9066

FAX #: 303-292-3512

AREA OF INVESTMENT REGION CONSIDERED: DENVER AND HOUSTON ONLY

MOST DESIRED INVESTMENTS IN FIELDS OF: TELECOMMUNICATIONS, HIGH TECHNOLOGY, BIOTECHNOLOGY, ELECTRONICS, LIFE SCIENCES, ENVIRONMENTAL, COMMUNICATIONS

POSSIBLE CONSIDERATION FOR INVESTMENT IN: NO OTHER FIELDS

NO INVESTMENT INTEREST WHATSOEVER IN: ALL OTHER FIELDS, NO REAL ESTATE

MINIMUM AND MAXIMUM INVESTMENT DOLLAR AMOUNT: $2,500,000+

HILL, CARMAN & WASHING

885 Arapahoe Ave.

Boulder, CO 80302

PHONE #: 303-442-5151

FAX #: 303-442-8525

AREA OF INVESTMENT REGION CONSIDERED: COLORADO ONLY

MOST DESIRED INVESTMENTS IN FIELDS OF: HIGH TECHNOLOGY, COMPUTER HARDWARE, COMPUTER SOFTWARE, TELECOMMUNICATIONS, ELECTRONICS

POSSIBLE CONSIDERATION FOR INVESTMENT IN: START-UP COMPANIES IN THESE FIELDS

NO INVESTMENT INTEREST WHATSOEVER IN: ALL OTHER FIELDS

MINIMUM AND MAXIMUM INVESTMENT DOLLAR AMOUNT: $250,000 to $500,000

CONSUMER VENTURE PARTNERS

Three Pickwick Plaza

Greenwich, CT 06830

PHONE #: 203-629-8800

FAX #: 203-629-2019

AREA OF INVESTMENT REGION CONSIDERED: UNITED STATES

MOST DESIRED INVESTMENTS IN FIELDS OF: CONSUMER PRODUCTS AND SERVICE COMPANIES-ONLY

POSSIBLE CONSIDERATION FOR INVESTMENT IN: NO OTHER FIELDS

NO INVESTMENT INTEREST WHATSOEVER IN: ALL OTHER FIELDS

MINIMUM AND MAXIMUM INVESTMENT DOLLAR AMOUNT: $1,000,000+

CANAAN PARTNERS

105 Rowayton Ave.

Rowayton, CT 06853

PHONE #: 203-855-0400

FAX #: 203-854-9117

AREA OF INVESTMENT REGION CONSIDERED: UNITED STATES

MOST DESIRED INVESTMENTS IN FIELDS OF: OPEN TO MANY INVESTMENTS IN MEDICAL AND HEALTH CARE FIELDS, BIOTECHNOLOGY, LIFE SCIENCES, MEDICINE, SERVICE COMPANIES, FINANCIAL SERVICE COMPANIES, DISTRIBUTION COMPANIES.

POSSIBLE CONSIDERATION FOR INVESTMENT IN: EARLY STAGE COMPANIES

NO INVESTMENT INTEREST WHATSOEVER IN: REAL ESTATE, OIL OR GAS, NO START-UP COMPANIES

MINIMUM AND MAXIMUM INVESTMENT DOLLAR AMOUNT: $2,500,000 to $15,000,000

OAK INVESTMENT PARTNERS

1 Gorham Island

Westport, CT 06880

PHONE #: 203-226-8346

FAX #: 203-227-0372

AREA OF INVESTMENT REGION CONSIDERED: UNITED STATES

MOST DESIRED INVESTMENTS IN FIELDS OF: MEDICAL PRODUCTS, SPECIALITY RETAILING, LIFE SCIENCES, MEDICINE, GENERAL HEALTH CARE

POSSIBLE CONSIDERATION FOR INVESTMENT IN: NO OTHER FIELDS

NO INVESTMENT INTEREST WHATSOEVER IN: ALL OTHER FIELDS

MINIMUM AND MAXIMUM INVESTMENT DOLLAR AMOUNT: $2,000,000+

PRINCE VENTURES

One Gorham Island

Westport, CT 06880

PHONE #: 203-227-8332

FAX #: 203-226-5302

AREA OF INVESTMENT REGION CONSIDERED: UNITED STATES

MOST DESIRED INVESTMENTS IN FIELDS OF: PHARMACEUTICAL, MEDICAL PRODUCTS, LIFE SCIENCES, BIOTECHNOLOGY

POSSIBLE CONSIDERATION FOR INVESTMENT IN: NO OTHER FIELDS

NO INVESTMENT INTEREST WHATSOEVER IN: ALL OTHER FIELDS

MINIMUM AND MAXIMUM INVESTMENT DOLLAR AMOUNT: $1,000,000+

OXFORD PARTNERS

315 Post Rd. West

Westport, CT 06880

PHONE #: 203-341-3300

FAX #: 203-341-3309

AREA OF INVESTMENT REGION CONSIDERED: UNITED STATES

MOST DESIRED INVESTMENTS IN FIELDS OF: MEDICAL PRODUCTS, BIOTECHNOLOGY, HEALTH CARE PRODUCTS, LIFE SCIENCES, MEDICINE, ENVIRONMENTAL

POSSIBLE CONSIDERATION FOR INVESTMENT IN: START-UP COMPANIES IN THESE FIELDS ONLY

NO INVESTMENT INTEREST WHATSOEVER IN: ALL OTHER FIELDS

MINIMUM AND MAXIMUM INVESTMENT DOLLAR AMOUNT: $1,000,000+

SAUGATUCK CAPITAL CO

One Canterbury Green

Stamford, CT 06901

PHONE #: 203-348-6669

FAX #: 203-324-6995

AREA OF INVESTMENT REGION CONSIDERED: UNITED STATES

MOST DESIRED INVESTMENTS IN FIELDS OF: OPEN TO MANY INVESTMENTS. HIGH TECHNOLOGY, COMPUTER PRODUCTS, INFORMATIONAL SERVICES, ELECTRONICS, LIFE SCIENCES, ENVIRONMENTAL, SERVICE COMPANIES, MANUFACTURING, COMMUNICATIONS

POSSIBLE CONSIDERATION FOR INVESTMENT IN: ESTABLISHED COMPANIES ONLY

NO INVESTMENT INTEREST WHATSOEVER IN: NO START-UP COMPANIES, REAL ESTATE, OIL OR GAS

MINIMUM AND MAXIMUM INVESTMENT DOLLAR AMOUNT: $2,000,000+

TSG VENTURES INC

1055 Washington Blvd.

10th Floor

Stamford, CT 06901

PHONE #: 203-363-5344

FAX #: 203-363-5340

AREA OF INVESTMENT REGION CONSIDERED: UNITED STATES

MOST DESIRED INVESTMENTS IN FIELDS OF: LOW TECHNOLOGY, MANUFACTURING, INDUSTRIAL PRODUCTS

POSSIBLE CONSIDERATION FOR INVESTMENT IN: ESTABLISHED COMPANIES IN THESE FIELDS ONLY

NO INVESTMENT INTEREST WHATSOEVER IN: ALL OTHER FIELDS

MINIMUM AND MAXIMUM INVESTMENT DOLLAR AMOUNT: $500,000+

SCHRODER VENTURES

1055 Washington Blvd.

5th Floor

Stamford, CT 06901

PHONE #: 203-324-7700

FAX #: 203-324-3636

AREA OF INVESTMENT REGION CONSIDERED: UNITED STATES

MOST DESIRED INVESTMENTS IN FIELDS OF: BIOTECHNOLOGY, MEDICAL SERVICES, HEALTH CARE PRODUCTS, MEDICAL PRODUCTS, MEDICAL ELECTRONICS, LIFE SCIENCES, MEDICINE

POSSIBLE CONSIDERATION FOR INVESTMENT IN: NO OTHER FIELDS

NO INVESTMENT INTEREST WHATSOEVER IN: ALL OTHER FIELDS

MINIMUM AND MAXIMUM INVESTMENT DOLLAR AMOUNT: $1,000,000 + VARIES

J.H. WHITNEY & CO.

177 Broad St.

Stamford, CT 06901

PHONE #: 203-973-1400

FAX #: 203-973-1422

AREA OF INVESTMENT REGION CONSIDERED: UNITED STATES

MOST DESIRED INVESTMENTS IN FIELDS OF: BIOTECHNOLOGY, MEDICAL PRODUCTS, HEALTH CARE, MEDICAL ELECTRONICS, LIFE SCIENCES, GENERAL HEALTH CARE PRODUCTS

POSSIBLE CONSIDERATION FOR INVESTMENT IN: NO OTHER FIELDS

NO INVESTMENT INTEREST WHATSOEVER IN: ALL OTHER FIELDS

MINIMUM AND MAXIMUM INVESTMENT DOLLAR AMOUNT: $2,000,000+

ALLIED CAPITAL ADVISERS, INC.

1666 K St. N.W.

Suite 901

Washington, D.C. 20006

PHONE #: 202-331-1112

FAX #: 202-659-2053

AREA OF INVESTMENT REGION CONSIDERED: UNITED STATES

MOST DESIRED INVESTMENTS IN FIELDS OF: ESTABLISH COMPANIES ONLY, OPEN TO MANY INVESTMENTS, HEALTH CARE, HEALTH PRODUCTS, HIGH TECHNOLOGY, TELE-COMMUNICATIONS

POSSIBLE CONSIDERATION FOR INVESTMENT IN: OPEN TO OTHER PROPOSALS

NO INVESTMENT INTEREST WHATSOEVER IN: START-UP COMPANIES, BIOTECHNOLOGY, REAL ESTATE, OIL OR GAS

MINIMUM AND MAXIMUM INVESTMENT DOLLAR AMOUNT: $1,000,000+

SOUTH ATLANTIC VENTURE FUND

614 West Bay St.

Suite 200

Tampa, FL 33606-2704

PHONE #: 813-253-2500

FAX #: 813-253-2360

AREA OF INVESTMENT REGION CONSIDERED: SOUTHEAST & TEXAS

MOST DESIRED INVESTMENTS IN FIELDS OF: OPEN TO MANY INVESTMENTS. HIGH TECHNOLOGY, COMPUTER PRODUCTS, BIOTECHNOLOGY, INFORMATIONAL SERVICES, ELECTRONICS, LIFE SCIENCES, MEDICINE, ENVIRONMENTAL, SERVICE COMPANIES, MANUFACTURING, COMMUNICATIONS

POSSIBLE CONSIDERATION FOR INVESTMENT IN: OPEN TO OTHER PROPOSALS

NO INVESTMENT INTEREST WHATSOEVER IN: REAL ESTATE, OIL OR GAS

MINIMUM AND MAXIMUM INVESTMENT DOLLAR AMOUNT: $1,000,000 to $5,000,000

ADVANCED TECH DEVELOPMENT FUND

1000 Abernathy Rd.

Suite 1420

Atlanta, GA 30328

PHONE #: 404-668-2333

FAX #:

AREA OF INVESTMENT REGION CONSIDERED: UNITED STATES

MOST DESIRED INVESTMENTS IN FIELDS OF: SPECIALIZED MOBILE RADIO, INFORMATION PROCESSING, COMPUTER SOFTWARE

POSSIBLE CONSIDERATION FOR INVESTMENT IN: NO OTHER FIELDS

NO INVESTMENT INTEREST WHATSOEVER IN: ALL OTHER FIELDS

MINIMUM AND MAXIMUM INVESTMENT DOLLAR AMOUNT: VARIES

ARETE VENTURES INC.

115 Perimeter Center Place

Suite 1140

Atlanta, GA 30346

PHONE #: 404-399-1660

FAX #: 404-399-1664

AREA OF INVESTMENT REGION CONSIDERED: UNITED STATES

MOST DESIRED INVESTMENTS IN FIELDS OF: COMPANIES DEALING WITH ELECTRIC AND GAS UTILITIES COMPANIES

POSSIBLE CONSIDERATION FOR INVESTMENT IN: RESEARCH AND DEVELOPMENT FOR TREATMENTS OR SERVICES FOR THE UTILITIES, ONLY

NO INVESTMENT INTEREST WHATSOEVER IN: ALL OTHER FIELDS

MINIMUM AND MAXIMUM INVESTMENT DOLLAR AMOUNT: VARIES

NORTH RIVERSIDE VENTURE GROUP

50 Technology Park

Norcross, GA 30092-4065

PHONE #: 404-446-5556

FAX #: 404-446-8627

AREA OF INVESTMENT REGION CONSIDERED: UNITED STATES

MOST DESIRED INVESTMENTS IN FIELDS OF: AUTOMOTIVE AFTER MARKET PRODUCTS AND SERVICES

POSSIBLE CONSIDERATION FOR INVESTMENT IN: NO OTHER FIELDS

NO INVESTMENT INTEREST WHATSOEVER IN: ALL OTHER FIELDS

MINIMUM AND MAXIMUM INVESTMENT DOLLAR AMOUNT: VARIES

INVESTAMERICA VENTURE GROUP INC

101 2nd St. S.E.

Suite 800

Cedar Rapids, IA 52401

PHONE #: 319-363-8249

FAX #: 319-363-9683

AREA OF INVESTMENT REGION CONSIDERED: MID WEST

MOST DESIRED INVESTMENTS IN FIELDS OF: MANUFACTURING, SERVICE COMPANIES, LIKES LATER STAGE COMPANIES

POSSIBLE CONSIDERATION FOR INVESTMENT IN: OPEN TO MANY FIELDS, SOME START-UP COMPANIES

NO INVESTMENT INTEREST WHATSOEVER IN: REAL ESTATE, OIL AND GAS

MINIMUM AND MAXIMUM INVESTMENT DOLLAR AMOUNT: $500,000+

EQUITY DYNAMICS INC.

2116 Financial Center

Des Moines, IA 50309

PHONE #: 515-244-5746

FAX #: 515-244-2346

AREA OF INVESTMENT REGION CONSIDERED: UNITED STATES

MOST DESIRED INVESTMENTS IN FIELDS OF: MEDICAL PRODUCTS, HEALTH CARE, BIOTECHNOLOGY, ARTIFICIAL INTELLIGENCE

POSSIBLE CONSIDERATION FOR INVESTMENT IN: RELATED FIELDS ONLY

NO INVESTMENT INTEREST WHATSOEVER IN: ALL OTHER FIELDS

MINIMUM AND MAXIMUM INVESTMENT DOLLAR AMOUNT: $500,000+

IOWA SEED CAPITAL CORP.

200 E. Grand Ave. Suite 160

Des Moines, IA 50309-1633

PHONE #: 515-242-4860

FAX #: 515-242-4722

AREA OF INVESTMENT REGION CONSIDERED: IOWA ONLY

MOST DESIRED INVESTMENTS IN FIELDS OF: OPEN TO MANY INVESTMENTS IN MANUFACTURING FIELDS

POSSIBLE CONSIDERATION FOR INVESTMENT IN: START-UPS

NO INVESTMENT INTEREST WHATSOEVER IN: REAL ESTATE, OIL, GAS

MINIMUM AND MAXIMUM INVESTMENT DOLLAR AMOUNT: $50,000 to $400,000

MARQUETTE VENTURE PARTNERS

520 Lake Cook Road

Suite 450

Deerfield, IL 60015

PHONE #: 708-940-1700

FAX #: 708-940-1724

AREA OF INVESTMENT REGION CONSIDERED: UNITED STATES

MOST DESIRED INVESTMENTS IN FIELDS OF: HEALTH CARE PRODUCTS, SPECIALITY RETAIL PRODUCTS, INFORMATION TECHNOLOGY, HEALTH CARE, BIOTECHNOLOGY, MEDICAL ELECTRONICS, LIFE SCIENCES

POSSIBLE CONSIDERATION FOR INVESTMENT IN: START-UP COMPANIES IN THESE FIELDS ONLY

NO INVESTMENT INTEREST WHATSOEVER IN: ALL OTHER FIELDS

MINIMUM AND MAXIMUM INVESTMENT DOLLAR AMOUNT: $2,000,000 to $5,000,000

COMDISCO VENTURE GROUP

611 N. River Rd.

Rosemont, IL 60018

PHONE #: 708-698-3000

FAX #: 708-518-5465

AREA OF INVESTMENT REGION CONSIDERED: UNITED STATES

MOST DESIRED INVESTMENTS IN FIELDS OF: OPEN TO MANY INVESTMENTS. HIGH TECHNOLOGY, COMPUTER PRODUCTS, BIOTECHNOLOGY, INFORMATIONAL SERVICES, ELECTRONICS, LIFE SCIENCES, MEDICINE, ENVIRONMENTAL, SERVICE COMPANIES, MANUFACTURING, COMMUNICATIONS

POSSIBLE CONSIDERATION FOR INVESTMENT IN: SOME START-UP COMPANIES, THEY WILL DO DEBT FINANCING

NO INVESTMENT INTEREST WHATSOEVER IN: REAL ESTATE, OIL OR GAS

MINIMUM AND MAXIMUM INVESTMENT DOLLAR AMOUNT: $250,000 + VARIES

VENTANA FINANCIAL RESOURCES INC

4 Market Square Ct.

Lake Forest, IL 60045

PHONE #: 708-234-3434

FAX #:

AREA OF INVESTMENT REGION CONSIDERED: MID WEST

MOST DESIRED INVESTMENTS IN FIELDS OF: BIOTECHNOLOGY, MEDICAL PRODUCTS, MEDICAL ELECTRONICS, LIFE SCIENCES

POSSIBLE CONSIDERATION FOR INVESTMENT IN: SOME START-UP COMPANIES IN THESE FIELDS ONLY

NO INVESTMENT INTEREST WHATSOEVER IN: ALL OTHER FIELDS

MINIMUM AND MAXIMUM INVESTMENT DOLLAR AMOUNT: $500,000 VARIES

ALLSTATE VENTURE CAPITAL

Allstate Plaza S. #G5D

Northbrook, IL 60062

PHONE #: 708-402-5681

FAX #: 708-402-0880

AREA OF INVESTMENT REGION CONSIDERED: UNITED STATES

MOST DESIRED INVESTMENTS IN FIELDS OF: OPEN TO MANY INVESTMENTS. HIGH TECHNOLOGY, COMPUTER HARDWARE AND SOFTWARE, INFORMATIONAL SERVICES, SERVICE COMPANIES, MANUFACTURING, MEDICAL CARE, MEDICAL PRODUCTS, LIFE SCIENCES, ENVIRONMENTAL

POSSIBLE CONSIDERATION FOR INVESTMENT IN: SOME START-UP COMPANIES, OPEN TO OTHER PROPOSALS

NO INVESTMENT INTEREST WHATSOEVER IN: REAL ESTATE, OIL AND GAS

MINIMUM AND MAXIMUM INVESTMENT DOLLAR AMOUNT: $500,000+

BOSTON CAPITAL VENTURES

205 N. Michigan Ave.

Suite 3911

Chicago, IL 60601

PHONE #: 312-946-1200

FAX #: 312-946-1103

AREA OF INVESTMENT REGION CONSIDERED: NORTHEAST UNITED STATES

MOST DESIRED INVESTMENTS IN FIELDS OF: HEALTH CARE, INFORMATIONAL SERVICES, COMMUNICATIONS, HEALTH CARE PRODUCTS, LIFE SCIENCES, MEDICINE

POSSIBLE CONSIDERATION FOR INVESTMENT IN: SOME START-UP COMPANIES, OPEN TO OTHER PROPOSALS

NO INVESTMENT INTEREST WHATSOEVER IN: REAL ESTATE, OIL OR GAS

MINIMUM AND MAXIMUM INVESTMENT DOLLAR AMOUNT: $500,000 to $5,000,000

ALPHA CAPITAL PARTNERS INC.

3 1st National Plaza

Suite 1400

Chicago, IL 60602

PHONE #: 312-214-3440

FAX #: 312-214-3376

AREA OF INVESTMENT REGION CONSIDERED: MID WEST

MOST DESIRED INVESTMENTS IN FIELDS OF: OPEN TO MANY INVESTMENTS, BIOTECHNOLOGY, HIGH TECHNOLOGY, ELECTRONICS, LIFE SCIENCES, ENVIRONMENTAL, MANUFACTURING

POSSIBLE CONSIDERATION FOR INVESTMENT IN: SOME START-UP COMPANIES

NO INVESTMENT INTEREST WHATSOEVER IN: ALL OTHER FIELDS

MINIMUM AND MAXIMUM INVESTMENT DOLLAR AMOUNT: $500,000+

SEARS INVESTMENT MANAGEMENT CO.

Xerox Center 55 W. Monroe

32nd Floor

Chicago, IL 60603

PHONE #: 312-875-0415

FAX #: 312-875-7529

AREA OF INVESTMENT REGION CONSIDERED: UNITED STATES

MOST DESIRED INVESTMENTS IN FIELDS OF: OPEN TO MANY INVESTMENTS. HIGH TECHNOLOGY, COMPUTER PRODUCTS, BIOTECHNOLOGY, ELECTRONICS, LIFE SCIENCES, MEDICAL PRODUCTS, ENVIRONMENTAL, INFORMATIONAL SERVICES, COMMUNICATIONS

POSSIBLE CONSIDERATION FOR INVESTMENT IN: ESTABLISHED COMPANIES ONLY

NO INVESTMENT INTEREST WHATSOEVER IN: ALL OTHER FIELDS. NO START-UP COMPANIES

MINIMUM AND MAXIMUM INVESTMENT DOLLAR AMOUNT: $750,000 to $2,500,000

CAPITAL HEALTH VENTURE PARTNERS

122 S. Michigan Ave.

Suite 1320

Chicago, IL 60603

PHONE #: 312-427-1227

FAX #: 312-427-1247

AREA OF INVESTMENT REGION CONSIDERED: UNITED STATES

MOST DESIRED INVESTMENTS IN FIELDS OF: MEDICAL PRODUCTS AND MEDICAL SERVICES

POSSIBLE CONSIDERATION FOR INVESTMENT IN: SOME START-UP COMPANIES IN MEDICAL FIELDS ONLY

NO INVESTMENT INTEREST WHATSOEVER IN: ALL OTHER FIELDS

MINIMUM AND MAXIMUM INVESTMENT DOLLAR AMOUNT: $500,000 to $2,000,000

ESSEX VENTURE PARTNERS

190 S. LaSalle St.

Suite 2800

Chicago, IL 60603

PHONE #: 312-444-6040

FAX #: 312-444-6034

AREA OF INVESTMENT REGION CONSIDERED: UNITED STATES

MOST DESIRED INVESTMENTS IN FIELDS OF: HEALTH CARE PRODUCTS ONLY

POSSIBLE CONSIDERATION FOR INVESTMENT IN: START-UP COMPANIES AND EARLY STAGE COMPANIES IN THESE FIELDS ONLY

NO INVESTMENT INTEREST WHATSOEVER IN: ALL OTHER FIELDS

MINIMUM AND MAXIMUM INVESTMENT DOLLAR AMOUNT: $500,000 to $3,000,000

FRONTENAC COMPANY

208 LaSalle St.

Suite 1900

Chicago, IL 60604

PHONE #: 312-368-0044

FAX #: 312-368-9520

AREA OF INVESTMENT REGION CONSIDERED: MIDWEST

MOST DESIRED INVESTMENTS IN FIELDS OF: INFORMATION SERVICES, CONSUMER PRODUCTS, MEDICAL HEALTH CARE, HEALTH CARE PRODUCTS, MEDICAL ELECTRONICS, LIFE SCIENCES, HEALTH CARE SERVICES, CONSUMER SERVICES

POSSIBLE CONSIDERATION FOR INVESTMENT IN: START-UP COMPANIES IN THESE FIELDS ONLY. NO OTHER FIELDS

NO INVESTMENT INTEREST WHATSOEVER IN: ALL OTHER FIELDS

MINIMUM AND MAXIMUM INVESTMENT DOLLAR AMOUNT: $500,000 to $25,000,000

WILLIAM BLAIR VENTURE PARTNERS

222 W. Adams, 33rd Floor

Chicago, IL 60606

PHONE #: 312-364-8250

FAX #: 312-236-1042

AREA OF INVESTMENT REGION CONSIDERED: UNITED STATES

MOST DESIRED INVESTMENTS IN FIELDS OF: OPEN TO MANY INVESTMENTS. HIGH TECHNOLOGY, COMPUTER HARDWARE AND SOFTWARE, ELECTRONICS, INFORMATIONAL SERVICES, SERVICE COMPANIES, MANUFACTURING, COMMUNICATIONS

POSSIBLE CONSIDERATION FOR INVESTMENT IN: SOME START-UP COMPANIES, OPEN TO OTHER PROPOSALS

NO INVESTMENT INTEREST WHATSOEVER IN: REAL ESTATE, OIL OR GAS, TRANSPORTATION

MINIMUM AND MAXIMUM INVESTMENT DOLLAR AMOUNT: $1,500,000 to $8,000,000

LA SALLE CAPITAL GROUP

70 W. Madison Street, Suite 5710

Chicago, IL 60602

PHONE #: 312-236-7041

FAX #: 312-236-0720

AREA OF INVESTMENT REGION CONSIDERED: UNITED STATES

MOST DESIRED INVESTMENTS IN FIELDS OF: ESTABLISHED CONSUMER MANUFACTURING COMPANIES. THEY WILL CONSIDER MOST COMPANIES THAT MANUFACTURE PRODUCTS FOR CONSUMERS

POSSIBLE CONSIDERATION FOR INVESTMENT IN: NO OTHER FIELDS

NO INVESTMENT INTEREST WHATSOEVER IN: ALL OTHER FIELDS

MINIMUM AND MAXIMUM INVESTMENT DOLLAR AMOUNT: $3,000,000+

AMERITECH DEVELOPMENT CORP.

30 S. Wacker Dr.

37th Floor

Chicago, IL 60606

PHONE #: 312-750-5083

FAX #:

AREA OF INVESTMENT REGION CONSIDERED: MID WEST

MOST DESIRED INVESTMENTS IN FIELDS OF: TELECOMMUNICATIONS, INFORMATION SERVICES, INFORMATION TECHNOLOGY, DATA COMMUNICATIONS

POSSIBLE CONSIDERATION FOR INVESTMENT IN: NO OTHER FIELDS

NO INVESTMENT INTEREST WHATSOEVER IN: ALL OTHER FIELDS

MINIMUM AND MAXIMUM INVESTMENT DOLLAR AMOUNT: $1,000,000+

FIRST ANALYSIS CORP.

233 S. Wacker Drive

Suite 9600

Chicago, IL 60606

PHONE #: 312-258-1400

FAX #: 312-258-0334

AREA OF INVESTMENT REGION CONSIDERED: UNITED STATES

MOST DESIRED INVESTMENTS IN FIELDS OF: ALL COMPANIES DEALING WITH ENVIRONMENTAL PRODUCTS AND SERVICES

POSSIBLE CONSIDERATION FOR INVESTMENT IN: START-UP COMPANIES BUT PREFERS ESTABLISHED COMPANIES

NO INVESTMENT INTEREST WHATSOEVER IN: ALL OTHER FIELDS

MINIMUM AND MAXIMUM INVESTMENT DOLLAR AMOUNT: $1,000,000+

PRINCE VENTURES

10 S. Wacker Drive.

Suite 2575

Chicago, IL 60606

PHONE #: 312-454-1408

FAX #: 312-454-9125

AREA OF INVESTMENT REGION CONSIDERED: UNITED STATES

MOST DESIRED INVESTMENTS IN FIELDS OF: PHARMACEUTICAL, MEDICAL PRODUCTS, MEDICAL HEALTH CARE, LIFE SCIENCES, BIOTECHNOLOGY

POSSIBLE CONSIDERATION FOR INVESTMENT IN: NO OTHER FIELDS

NO INVESTMENT INTEREST WHATSOEVER IN: ALL OTHER FIELDS

MINIMUM AND MAXIMUM INVESTMENT DOLLAR AMOUNT: $1,000,000+

IEG VENTURE MANAGEMENT, INC.

10 S. Riverside Plaza

14th Floor

Chicago, IL 60606

PHONE #: 312-993-7500

FAX #: 312-454-0369

AREA OF INVESTMENT REGION CONSIDERED: UNITED STATES

MOST DESIRED INVESTMENTS IN FIELDS OF: COMPUTER SOFTWARE, MEDICAL HEALTH CARE PRODUCTS, MEDICAL HEALTH CARE SERVICES, BIOTECHNOLOGY

POSSIBLE CONSIDERATION FOR INVESTMENT IN: START-UP COMPANIES IN THESE FIELDS ONLY

NO INVESTMENT INTEREST WHATSOEVER IN: ALL OTHER FIELDS

MINIMUM AND MAXIMUM INVESTMENT DOLLAR AMOUNT: $250,000 + VARIES

MIDWEST MEZZINE FUND

141 W. Jackson Blvd.

Suite 2900

Chicago, IL 60604

PHONE #: 312-341-7964

FAX #: 312-341-7916

AREA OF INVESTMENT REGION CONSIDERED: MIDWEST UNITED STATES

MOST DESIRED INVESTMENTS IN FIELDS OF: ESTABLISHED COMPANIES WITH OVER $2,000,000 IN OPERATING PROFIT PER YEAR, CONSUMER MANUFACTURING COMPANIES, DISTRIBUTION COMPANIES, SPECIALTY RETAILING COMPANIES

POSSIBLE CONSIDERATION FOR INVESTMENT IN: NO OTHER FIELDS

NO INVESTMENT INTEREST WHATSOEVER IN: HIGH TECHNOLOGY, REAL ESTATE, OIL, GAS OR START-UP COMPANIES

MINIMUM AND MAXIMUM INVESTMENT DOLLAR AMOUNT: $2,000,000 to $6,000,000

APEX INVESTMENTS PARTNERS

233 S. Wacker Dr.

Suite 9600

Chicago, IL 60606

PHONE #: 312-258-0320

FAX #: 312-258-0334

AREA OF INVESTMENT REGION CONSIDERED: UNITED STATES

MOST DESIRED INVESTMENTS IN FIELDS OF: CONSUMER GOODS, TELECOMMUNICATIONS, CONSUMER ELECTRONICS, ENVIRONMENTAL, HEALTH CARE PRODUCTS

POSSIBLE CONSIDERATION FOR INVESTMENT IN: NO OTHER FIELDS, INCLUDING START-UP COMPANIES

NO INVESTMENT INTEREST WHATSOEVER IN: ALL OTHER FIELDS

MINIMUM AND MAXIMUM INVESTMENT DOLLAR AMOUNT: $500,000+

MESIROW PRIVATE EQUITY INVESTMENTS

350 N. Clark St.

Chicago, IL 60610

PHONE #: 312-670-6099

FAX #: 312-670-6211

AREA OF INVESTMENT REGION CONSIDERED: UNITED STATES

MOST DESIRED INVESTMENTS IN FIELDS OF: MUST HAVE $8,000,000 IN REVENUES TO BE CONSIDERED FOR INVESTMENT. SERVICE COMPANIES, MANUFACTURING COMPANIES, DISTRIBUTION COMPANIES

POSSIBLE CONSIDERATION FOR INVESTMENT IN: NO OTHER FIELDS

NO INVESTMENT INTEREST WHATSOEVER IN: ALL OTHER FIELDS

MINIMUM AND MAXIMUM INVESTMENT DOLLAR AMOUNT: $10,000,000+

CONTINENTAL ILLINOIS VENTURE CORP

231 S. LaSalle St.

Chicago, IL 60697

PHONE #: 312-828-8021

FAX #: 312-987-0887

AREA OF INVESTMENT REGION CONSIDERED: UNITED STATES

MOST DESIRED INVESTMENTS IN FIELDS OF: ONLY LOOKING FOR BUYOUT SITUATIONS

POSSIBLE CONSIDERATION FOR INVESTMENT IN: NO OTHERS

NO INVESTMENT INTEREST WHATSOEVER IN: ALL OTHERS

MINIMUM AND MAXIMUM INVESTMENT DOLLAR AMOUNT: $5,000,000 to $20,000,000

BRINSON PARTNERS, INC.

209 S. LaSalle St.

Suite 114

Chicago, IL 60604-1295

PHONE #: 312-220-7100

FAX #: 312-220-7100

AREA OF INVESTMENT REGION CONSIDERED: UNITED STATES

MOST DESIRED INVESTMENTS IN FIELDS OF: OPEN TO MANY INVESTMENTS. HIGH TECHNOLOGY, COMPUTER PRODUCTS, ELECTRONICS, LIFE SCIENCES, ENVIRONMENTAL, BIOTECHNOLOGY, INFORMATIONAL SERVICES, SERVICE COMPANIES, MANUFACTURING, COMMUNICATIONS

POSSIBLE CONSIDERATION FOR INVESTMENT IN: OTHER LATER STAGE COMPANIES, OPEN TO OTHER PROPOSALS

NO INVESTMENT INTEREST WHATSOEVER IN: REAL ESTATE, OIL OR GAS

MINIMUM AND MAXIMUM INVESTMENT DOLLAR AMOUNT: $500,000 to $20,000,000

MASIROW FINANCIAL PRIVATE EQUITY DIVISION

350 N. Clark Street

Chicago, IL 60610

PHONE #: 312-670-6099

FAX #: 312-670-6211

AREA OF INVESTMENT REGION CONSIDERED: UNITED STATES

MOST DESIRED INVESTMENTS IN FIELDS OF: OPEN TO MANY DIFFERENT COMPANIES. MUST BE ESTABLISHED COMPANIES, $10,000,000 MINIMUM SALES

POSSIBLE CONSIDERATION FOR INVESTMENT IN: NO OTHER FIELDS

NO INVESTMENT INTEREST WHATSOEVER IN: NO EARLY STAGE OR START-UP COMPANIES

MINIMUM AND MAXIMUM INVESTMENT DOLLAR AMOUNT: $5,000,000 to $10,000,000

CARDINAL VENTURES LLC

8910 Purdue Rd.

Suite 690

Indianapolis, IN 46268

PHONE #: 317-228-5070

FAX #: 317-228-5080

AREA OF INVESTMENT REGION CONSIDERED: MIDWEST

MOST DESIRED INVESTMENTS IN FIELDS OF: OPEN TO MANY INVESTMENTS IN LOW TECHNOLOGY FIELDS AND MANUFACTURING

POSSIBLE CONSIDERATION FOR INVESTMENT IN: SOME START-UP COMPANIES IN THESE FIELDS

NO INVESTMENT INTEREST WHATSOEVER IN: NO HIGH TECHNOLOGY OR BIOTECHNOLOGY COMPANIES

MINIMUM AND MAXIMUM INVESTMENT DOLLAR AMOUNT: $500,000+

FIRST SOURCE CAPITAL CORP

100 N. Michigan

South Bend, IN 46634

PHONE #: 219-235-2180

FAX #: 219-235-2719

AREA OF INVESTMENT REGION CONSIDERED: MID WEST, INDIANA

MOST DESIRED INVESTMENTS IN FIELDS OF: HIGH TECHNOLOGY FIELDS AND MANUFACTURING ONLY

POSSIBLE CONSIDERATION FOR INVESTMENT IN: ESTABLISHED COMPANIES, WORKS WITH S.B.A., FOR SMALLER LOANS

NO INVESTMENT INTEREST WHATSOEVER IN: START-UP COMPANIES, ALL OTHER FIELDS

MINIMUM AND MAXIMUM INVESTMENT DOLLAR AMOUNT: $200,000+

INDIANA BUSINESS MODERNIZATION & TECH CORP

1 N. Capital Ave.

Suite 925

Indianapolis, IN 46260-1809

PHONE #: 317-635-3058

FAX #: 317-231-7095

AREA OF INVESTMENT REGION CONSIDERED: INDIANA

MOST DESIRED INVESTMENTS IN FIELDS OF: NEW TECHNOLOGY, CONSUMER PRODUCTS, COMPUTER SOFTWARE, ELECTRONICS, ENVIRONMENTAL, MANUFACTURING

POSSIBLE CONSIDERATION FOR INVESTMENT IN: OTHER INVESTMENTS, AND SOME START-UP COMPANIES

NO INVESTMENT INTEREST WHATSOEVER IN: REAL ESTATE AND RETAIL

MINIMUM AND MAXIMUM INVESTMENT DOLLAR AMOUNT: $50,000 to $500,000

KANSAS VENTURE CAPITAL INC.

6700 Antioch

Suite 460

Overland Park, KS 66204

PHONE #: 913-262-7117

FAX #: 913-262-3509

AREA OF INVESTMENT REGION CONSIDERED: KANSAS ONLY

MOST DESIRED INVESTMENTS IN FIELDS OF: MANY FIELDS IN MANUFACTURING ONLY

POSSIBLE CONSIDERATION FOR INVESTMENT IN: SOME START-UP COMPANIES

NO INVESTMENT INTEREST WHATSOEVER IN: RETAIL, REAL ESTATE, OIL OR GAS

MINIMUM AND MAXIMUM INVESTMENT DOLLAR AMOUNT: $250,000 to $1,000,000+

KENTUCKY HIGHLANDS INVESTMENTS

362 Old Whitley Rd.

London, KY 40741

PHONE #: 606-864-5175

FAX #: 606-864-5194

AREA OF INVESTMENT REGION CONSIDERED: KENTUCKY COMPANIES ONLY

MOST DESIRED INVESTMENTS IN FIELDS OF: OPEN TO MANY FIELDS FOR COMPANIES IN KENTUCKY

POSSIBLE CONSIDERATION FOR INVESTMENT IN: SOME START-UP COMPANIES

NO INVESTMENT INTEREST WHATSOEVER IN: REAL ESTATE, OIL GAS OR MINES

MINIMUM AND MAXIMUM INVESTMENT DOLLAR AMOUNT: $250,000 + VARIES

PREMIERE VENTURE CAPITAL CORP

451 Florida St.

Baton Rouge, LA 70801

PHONE #: 504-332-4421

FAX #: 504-332-4421

AREA OF INVESTMENT REGION CONSIDERED: LOUISIANA ONLY

MOST DESIRED INVESTMENTS IN FIELDS OF: OPEN TO MANY INVESTMENTS. HIGH TECHNOLOGY, COMPUTER PRODUCTS, BIOTECHNOLOGY, INFORMATIONAL SERVICES, ELECTRONICS, LIFE SCIENCES, ENVIRONMENTAL, SERVICE COMPANIES, MANUFACTURING, COMMUNICATIONS

POSSIBLE CONSIDERATION FOR INVESTMENT IN: MANY ESTABLISHED COMPANIES

NO INVESTMENT INTEREST WHATSOEVER IN: START UP COMPANIES, REAL ESTATE, OIL OR GAS

MINIMUM AND MAXIMUM INVESTMENT DOLLAR AMOUNT: $500,000 to $2,000,000

ARETE VENTURES INC

6110 Executive Blvd.

Suite 1040

Rockville, MD 20852

PHONE #: 301-881-2555

FAX #: 301-770-2877

AREA OF INVESTMENT REGION CONSIDERED: UNITED STATES

MOST DESIRED INVESTMENTS IN FIELDS OF: COMPANIES DEALING WITH ELECTRIC AND GAS UTILITY COMPANIES

POSSIBLE CONSIDERATION FOR INVESTMENT IN: RESEARCH AND DEVELOPMENT FOR TREATMENTS OR SERVICES FOR THE UTILITIES ONLY

NO INVESTMENT INTEREST WHATSOEVER IN: ALL OTHER FIELDS

MINIMUM AND MAXIMUM INVESTMENT DOLLAR AMOUNT: VARIES

GROTECH CAPITAL GROUP, INC.

9690 Deereco Rd.

Timonium, MD 21093

PHONE #: 410-560-2000

FAX #: 410-560-1910

AREA OF INVESTMENT REGION CONSIDERED: EAST COAST

MOST DESIRED INVESTMENTS IN FIELDS OF: OPEN TO MANY INVESTMENTS. HIGH TECHNOLOGY, COMPUTER PRODUCTS, BIOTECHNOLOGY, INFORMATIONAL SERVICES, SERVICE COMPANIES, ELECTRONICS, LIFE SCIENCES, ENVIRONMENTAL MANUFACTURING, COMMUNICATIONS

POSSIBLE CONSIDERATION FOR INVESTMENT IN: SOME START-UP COMPANIES, OPEN TO OTHER PROPOSALS

NO INVESTMENT INTEREST WHATSOEVER IN: REAL ESTATE, OIL OR GAS

MINIMUM AND MAXIMUM INVESTMENT DOLLAR AMOUNT: $500,000+

ABS VENTURES LIMITED PARTNERSHIP

10 North Calvert St.

Suite 735

Baltimore, MD 21202

PHONE #: 410-783-3263

FAX #: 410-347-2963

AREA OF INVESTMENT REGION CONSIDERED: UNITED STATES

MOST DESIRED INVESTMENTS IN FIELDS OF: HEALTH CARE SERVICES, HEALTH CARE PRODUCTS, DATA COMMUNICATIONS, INFORMATIONAL SERVICES

POSSIBLE CONSIDERATION FOR INVESTMENT IN: START-UP COMPANIES, TELE-COMMUNICATIONS, HIGH TECHNOLOGY

NO INVESTMENT INTEREST WHATSOEVER IN: REAL ESTATE, GAS, OIL

MINIMUM AND MAXIMUM INVESTMENT DOLLAR AMOUNT: $200,000 to over $1,000,000

NEW ENTERPRISE ASSOC.

1119 St. Paul St.

Baltimore, MD 21202

PHONE #: 410-244-0115

FAX #: 410-752-7721

AREA OF INVESTMENT REGION CONSIDERED: UNITED STATES

MOST DESIRED INVESTMENTS IN FIELDS OF: HIGH TECHNOLOGY, COMPUTER PRODUCTS, BIOTECHNOLOGY, INFORMATIONAL SERVICES, ELECTRONICS, LIFE SCIENCES, ENVIRONMENTAL, COMMUNICATIONS

POSSIBLE CONSIDERATION FOR INVESTMENT IN: SOME START-UP COMPANIES

NO INVESTMENT INTEREST WHATSOEVER IN: ALL OTHER FIELDS

MINIMUM AND MAXIMUM INVESTMENT DOLLAR AMOUNT: $500,000+

MARYLAND VENTURE CAPITAL TRUST

29 W. Susquehanna Ave.

4th Floor

Baltimore, MD 21204

PHONE #: 410-828-7292

FAX #: 410-828-6084

AREA OF INVESTMENT REGION CONSIDERED: MARYLAND, VIRGINIA, PENNSYLVANIA

MOST DESIRED INVESTMENTS IN FIELDS OF: OPEN TO MANY INVESTMENTS. HIGH TECHNOLOGY, BIOTECHNOLOGY, ELECTRONICS, LIFE SCIENCES, ENVIRONMENTAL LOW TECHNOLOGY, MANUFACTURING

POSSIBLE CONSIDERATION FOR INVESTMENT IN: ESTABLISHED COMPANIES ONLY, NO START-UP COMPANIES

NO INVESTMENT INTEREST WHATSOEVER IN: REAL ESTATE AND ALL OTHER FIELDS

MINIMUM AND MAXIMUM INVESTMENT DOLLAR AMOUNT: $500,000+ $4,000,000

PALMER PARTNERS

300 Unicorn Park Dr.

Woburn, MA 01801

PHONE #: 617-933-5445

FAX #: 617-933-0698

AREA OF INVESTMENT REGION CONSIDERED: UNITED STATES

MOST DESIRED INVESTMENTS IN FIELDS OF: OPEN TO MANY INVESTMENTS. HIGH TECHNOLOGY, COMPUTER PRODUCTS, BIOTECHNOLOGY, INFORMATIONAL SERVICES, ELECTRONICS, LIFE SCIENCES, ENVIRONMENTAL, SERVICE COMPANIES, MANUFACTURING, COMMUNICATIONS

POSSIBLE CONSIDERATION FOR INVESTMENT IN: START-UP COMPANIES IN THESE FIELDS ONLY

NO INVESTMENT INTEREST WHATSOEVER IN: REAL ESTATE, OIL OR GAS

MINIMUM AND MAXIMUM INVESTMENT DOLLAR AMOUNT: $250,000+

CP VENTURES

25 Burlington Mall Rd.

Burlington, MA 01803

PHONE #: 617-272-2760

FAX #: 617-272-2497

AREA OF INVESTMENT REGION CONSIDERED: UNITED STATES

MOST DESIRED INVESTMENTS IN FIELDS OF: COMPUTER SOFTWARE

POSSIBLE CONSIDERATION FOR INVESTMENT IN: NO OTHER FIELDS

NO INVESTMENT INTEREST WHATSOEVER IN: ALL OTHER FIELDS

MINIMUM AND MAXIMUM INVESTMENT DOLLAR AMOUNT: $250,000 to $1,000,000

BOSTON CAPITAL VENTURES

Old City Hall

45 School St.

Boston, MA 02108

PHONE #: 617-227-6550

FAX #: 617-227-3847

AREA OF INVESTMENT REGION CONSIDERED: NORTHEAST UNITED STATES

MOST DESIRED INVESTMENTS IN FIELDS OF: MEDICAL HEALTH CARE PRODUCTS, INFORMATIONAL SERVICES, COMMUNICATIONS, HEALTH CARE SERVICES, LIFE SCIENCES

POSSIBLE CONSIDERATION FOR INVESTMENT IN: SOME START-UP COMPANIES, OPEN TO OTHER PROPOSALS

NO INVESTMENT INTEREST WHATSOEVER IN: REAL ESTATE, OIL OR GAS

MINIMUM AND MAXIMUM INVESTMENT DOLLAR AMOUNT: $500,000 to $5,000,000

SUMMIT PARTNERS

One Boston Place

34th Floor

Boston, MA 02108

PHONE #: 617-742-5500

FAX #: 617-742-6138

AREA OF INVESTMENT REGION CONSIDERED: UNITED STATES

MOST DESIRED INVESTMENTS IN FIELDS OF: OPEN TO MANY INVESTMENTS. HIGH TECHNOLOGY, COMPUTER PRODUCTS, BIOTECHNOLOGY, INFORMATIONAL SERVICES, SERVICE COMPANIES, MANUFACTURING, COMMUNICATIONS, ELECTRONICS, LIFE SCIENCES, ENVIRONMENTAL

POSSIBLE CONSIDERATION FOR INVESTMENT IN: OPEN TO OTHER PROPOSALS

NO INVESTMENT INTEREST WHATSOEVER IN: REAL ESTATE, OIL & GAS

MINIMUM AND MAXIMUM INVESTMENT DOLLAR AMOUNT: $2,000,000 to $20,000,000

ADVANCED TECHNOLOGY VENTURES

10 Post Office Square

Suite 970

Boston, MA 02109

PHONE #: 617-423-4050

FAX #: 617-423-4573

AREA OF INVESTMENT REGION CONSIDERED: UNITED STATES

MOST DESIRED INVESTMENTS IN FIELDS OF: HIGH TECHNOLOGY, BIOTECHNOLOGY, HIGH PRIORITY TECHNOLOGY PRODUCTS ONLY

POSSIBLE CONSIDERATION FOR INVESTMENT IN: START-UP COMPANIES IN THESE FIELDS ONLY

NO INVESTMENT INTEREST WHATSOEVER IN: ALL OTHERS FIELDS

MINIMUM AND MAXIMUM INVESTMENT DOLLAR AMOUNT: $500,000 to $2,000,000

ABS VENTURES LIMITED PARTNERSHIP

160 State St.

Boston, MA 02109

PHONE #: 617-248-9421

FAX #: 617-683-0384

AREA OF INVESTMENT REGION CONSIDERED: UNITED STATES

MOST DESIRED INVESTMENTS IN FIELDS OF: HEALTH CARE, HEALTH CARE PRODUCTS, DATA COMMUNICATIONS

POSSIBLE CONSIDERATION FOR INVESTMENT IN: START-UP COMPANIES, TELECOMMUNICATIONS, HIGH TECHNOLOGY PRODUCTS, ELECTRONICS

NO INVESTMENT INTEREST WHATSOEVER IN: REAL ESTATE, GAS, OIL

MINIMUM AND MAXIMUM INVESTMENT DOLLAR AMOUNT: $200,000 to $1,000,000+

PIONEER CAPITAL CORP

60 State St.

Boston, MA 02109

PHONE #: 617-422-4754

FAX #: 617-742-7315

AREA OF INVESTMENT REGION CONSIDERED: NEW ENGLAND

MOST DESIRED INVESTMENTS IN FIELDS OF: OPEN TO MANY INVESTMENTS. HIGH TECHNOLOGY, COMPUTER PRODUCTS, INFORMATIONAL SERVICES, SERVICE COMPANIES, MANUFACTURING, COMMUNICATIONS, ELECTRONICS, ENVIRONMENTAL

POSSIBLE CONSIDERATION FOR INVESTMENT IN: START-UP COMPANIES IN THESE FIELDS ONLY

NO INVESTMENT INTEREST WHATSOEVER IN: REAL ESTATE, OIL OR GAS

MINIMUM AND MAXIMUM INVESTMENT DOLLAR AMOUNT: $250,000+

MORGAN, HOLLAND VENTURES

One Liberty Sq.

2nd Floor

Boston, MA 02109

PHONE #: 617-423-1765

FAX #: 617-338-4362

AREA OF INVESTMENT REGION CONSIDERED: MIDWEST & NORTH EAST

MOST DESIRED INVESTMENTS IN FIELDS OF: HIGH TECHNOLOGY, BIOTECHNOLOGY, INVESTMENTS IN THESE FIELDS ONLY

POSSIBLE CONSIDERATION FOR INVESTMENT IN: NO OTHER FIELDS

NO INVESTMENT INTEREST WHATSOEVER IN: ALL OTHER FIELDS

MINIMUM AND MAXIMUM INVESTMENT DOLLAR AMOUNT: $500,000 to $1,000,000+

AMERICAN RESEARCH & DEVELOPMENT CORP.

45 Milk St.

Boston, MA 02109

PHONE #: 617-423-7500

FAX #: 617-423-9655

AREA OF INVESTMENT REGION CONSIDERED: UNITED STATES

MOST DESIRED INVESTMENTS IN FIELDS OF: HIGH TECHNOLOGY, COMPUTER HARDWARE, COMPUTER SOFTWARE, ELECTRONICS

POSSIBLE CONSIDERATION FOR INVESTMENT IN: SOME START-UP COMPANIES

NO INVESTMENT INTEREST WHATSOEVER IN: ALL OTHER FIELDS

MINIMUM AND MAXIMUM INVESTMENT DOLLAR AMOUNT: $100,000 to $1,000,000.

CHARLES RIVER VENTURES

10 Post Office Square

Suite 1330

Boston, MA 02109

PHONE #: 617-292-7717

FAX #: 617-292-7718

AREA OF INVESTMENT REGION CONSIDERED: UNITED STATES

MOST DESIRED INVESTMENTS IN FIELDS OF: OPEN TO MANY INVESTMENTS. THEY LIKE EARLY STAGE COMPANIES, LIFE SCIENCES, COMPUTER SOFTWARE, INFORMATIONAL SERVICES, COMMUNICATIONS

POSSIBLE CONSIDERATION FOR INVESTMENT IN: EARLY STAGE COMPANIES, OPEN TO OTHER PROPOSALS

NO INVESTMENT INTEREST WHATSOEVER IN: REAL ESTATE, OIL OR GAS

MINIMUM AND MAXIMUM INVESTMENT DOLLAR AMOUNT: $500,000 to $1,500,000

HAMBRO INTERNATIONAL EQUITY PARTNERS

160 State Street

Boston, MA 02109

PHONE #: 617-523-7767

FAX #: 617-290-0999

AREA OF INVESTMENT REGION CONSIDERED: UNITED STATES

MOST DESIRED INVESTMENTS IN FIELDS OF: OPEN TO MANY INVESTMENTS. HIGH TECHNOLOGY, COMPUTER PRODUCTS, BIOTECHNOLOGY, INFORMATIONAL SERVICES, ELECTRONICS, LIFE SCIENCES, ENVIRONMENTAL, SERVICE COMPANIES, MANUFACTURING, COMMUNICATIONS

POSSIBLE CONSIDERATION FOR INVESTMENT IN: OPEN TO OTHER PROPOSALS

NO INVESTMENT INTEREST WHATSOEVER IN: REAL ESTATE, OIL OR GAS

MINIMUM AND MAXIMUM INVESTMENT DOLLAR AMOUNT: $2,000,000 to $5,000,000

FIDELITY CAPITAL

82 Devonshire St-R25C

Boston, MA 02109

PHONE #: 617-563-9106

FAX #: 617-476-6105

AREA OF INVESTMENT REGION CONSIDERED: UNITED STATES

MOST DESIRED INVESTMENTS IN FIELDS OF: OPEN TO MANY INVESTMENTS. HIGH TECHNOLOGY, COMPUTER PRODUCTS, BIOTECHNOLOGY, INFORMATIONAL SERVICES, SERVICE COMPANIES, ELECTRONICS, LIFE SCIENCES, ENVIRONMENTAL, MANUFACTURING, COMMUNICATIONS

POSSIBLE CONSIDERATION FOR INVESTMENT IN: SOME START-UP COMPANIES, OPEN TO OTHER PROPOSALS

NO INVESTMENT INTEREST WHATSOEVER IN: REAL ESTATE, OIL OR GAS

MINIMUM AND MAXIMUM INVESTMENT DOLLAR AMOUNT: $500,000+

TVM TECHNO VENTURE MGMT

101 Arch St.

Suite 1950

Boston, MA 02110

PHONE #: 617-345-9320

FAX #: 617-345-9377

AREA OF INVESTMENT REGION CONSIDERED: UNITED STATES

MOST DESIRED INVESTMENTS IN FIELDS OF: OPEN TO MANY INVESTMENTS. HIGH TECHNOLOGY, COMPUTER PRODUCTS, BIOTECHNOLOGY, INFORMATIONAL SERVICES, SERVICE COMPANIES, MANUFACTURING, COMMUNICATIONS, ELECTRONICS

POSSIBLE CONSIDERATION FOR INVESTMENT IN: OPEN TO OTHER PROPOSALS

NO INVESTMENT INTEREST WHATSOEVER IN: REAL ESTATE, OIL OR GAS

MINIMUM AND MAXIMUM INVESTMENT DOLLAR AMOUNT: $500,000 to $1,000,000

ADVENT INTERNATIONAL CORP.

101 Federal St.

Boston, MA 02110

PHONE #: 617-951-9400

FAX #: 617-951-0566

AREA OF INVESTMENT REGION CONSIDERED: UNITED STATES

MOST DESIRED INVESTMENTS IN FIELDS OF: BIOTECHNOLOGY, MEDICAL HEALTH CARE PRODUCTS, COMPUTER SOFTWARE, INFORMATIONAL SERVICES, TELECOMMUNICATIONS, HIGH TECHNOLOGY, ELECTRONICS, LIFE SCIENCES

POSSIBLE CONSIDERATION FOR INVESTMENT IN: INDUSTRIAL PRODUCTS, CHEMICALS, ENVIRONMENTAL, SOME START-UP COMPANIES, OPEN TO OTHER PROPOSALS.

NO INVESTMENT INTEREST WHATSOEVER IN: REAL ESTATE, OIL OR GAS.

MINIMUM AND MAXIMUM INVESTMENT DOLLAR AMOUNT: $1,000,000 to $15,000,000.

BANCBOSTON VENTURES, INC.

100 Federal St.

Boston, MA 02110

PHONE #: 617-434-2442

FAX #: 617-434-1383

AREA OF INVESTMENT REGION CONSIDERED: UNITED STATES

MOST DESIRED INVESTMENTS IN FIELDS OF: BIOTECHNOLOGY, HIGH TECHNOLOGY, T.V., RADIO, TELECOMMUNICATIONS, COMPUTER HARDWARE, COMPUTER SOFTWARE, ELECTRONICS, LIFE SCIENCES, ENVIRONMENTAL, COMMUNICATIONS

POSSIBLE CONSIDERATION FOR INVESTMENT IN: START-UP COMPANIES, OPEN TO OTHER PROPOSALS

NO INVESTMENT INTEREST WHATSOEVER IN: REAL ESTATE, OIL & GAS

MINIMUM AND MAXIMUM INVESTMENT DOLLAR AMOUNT: $500,000 to $3,000,000

HIGHLAND CAPITAL PARTNERS

One International Place

Boston, MA 02110

PHONE #: 617-330-8765

FAX #: 617-330-8768

AREA OF INVESTMENT REGION CONSIDERED: UNITED STATES

MOST DESIRED INVESTMENTS IN FIELDS OF: HEALTH CARE PRODUCTS, TELECOMMUNICATIONS, HIGH TECHNOLOGY. BIOTECHNOLOGY, ELECTRONICS, LIFE SCIENCES, MEDICINE, MEDICAL PRODUCTS

POSSIBLE CONSIDERATION FOR INVESTMENT IN: OTHER SIMILAR COMPANIES IN THESE FIELDS

NO INVESTMENT INTEREST WHATSOEVER IN: REAL ESTATE, OIL, GAS. ALL OTHER FIELDS

MINIMUM AND MAXIMUM INVESTMENT DOLLAR AMOUNT: $500,000+

MATRIX PARTNERS

One International Place

Suite 3250

Boston, MA 02110

PHONE #: 617-345-6740

FAX #: 617-345-6773

AREA OF INVESTMENT REGION CONSIDERED: UNITED STATES

MOST DESIRED INVESTMENTS IN FIELDS OF: HIGH TECHNOLOGY, COMMUNICATIONS, COMPUTER SOFTWARE

POSSIBLE CONSIDERATION FOR INVESTMENT IN: START-UP COMPANIES IN THESE FIELDS ONLY

NO INVESTMENT INTEREST WHATSOEVER IN: ALL OTHER FIELDS

MINIMUM AND MAXIMUM INVESTMENT DOLLAR AMOUNT: $1,000,000+

THE VENTURE CAPITAL FUND OF NEW ENGLAND

160 Federal St.
23rd Floor
Boston, MA 02110
PHONE #: 617-439-4646
FAX #: 617-439-4652

AREA OF INVESTMENT REGION CONSIDERED: UNITED STATES

MOST DESIRED INVESTMENTS IN FIELDS OF: HIGH TECHNOLOGY, LEADING EDGE TECHNOLOGY, BIOTECHNOLOGY

POSSIBLE CONSIDERATION FOR INVESTMENT IN: NO OTHER FIELDS

NO INVESTMENT INTEREST WHATSOEVER IN: ALL OTHER FIELDS

MINIMUM AND MAXIMUM INVESTMENT DOLLAR AMOUNT: $500,000+

HANDCOCK VENTURE PARTNERS

One Financial Center

44th Floor

Boston, MA 02111

PHONE #: 617-348-3707

FAX #: 617-350-0305

AREA OF INVESTMENT REGION CONSIDERED: UNITED STATES

MOST DESIRED INVESTMENTS IN FIELDS OF: OPEN TO MANY INVESTMENTS. HIGH TECHNOLOGY, COMPUTER PRODUCTS, BIOTECHNOLOGY, INFORMATIONAL SERVICES, SERVICE COMPANIES, ELECTRONICS, LIFE SCIENCES, ENVIRONMENTAL, MANUFACTURING, COMMUNICATIONS

POSSIBLE CONSIDERATION FOR INVESTMENT IN: OPEN TO OTHER PROPOSALS

NO INVESTMENT INTEREST WHATSOEVER IN: REAL ESTATE, OIL OR GAS

MINIMUM AND MAXIMUM INVESTMENT DOLLAR AMOUNT: $3,000,000+

BATTERY VENTURES, L.P.

200 Portland St.

Boston, MA 02114

PHONE #: 617-367-1011

FAX #: 617-367-1070

AREA OF INVESTMENT REGION CONSIDERED: UNITED STATES

MOST DESIRED INVESTMENTS IN FIELDS OF: COMPUTER SOFTWARE, INFORMATIONAL SERVICES, COMMUNICATIONS, DATA COMMUNICATIONS, TELECOMMUNICATIONS

POSSIBLE CONSIDERATION FOR INVESTMENT IN: SOME START-UP COMPANIES IN THESE FIELDS

NO INVESTMENT INTEREST WHATSOEVER IN: ALL OTHER FIELDS

MINIMUM AND MAXIMUM INVESTMENT DOLLAR AMOUNT: $500,000 to $10,000,000

HLM MANAGEMENT COMPANY

222 Berkeley St.

Boston, MA 02116

PHONE #: 617-266-0030

FAX #: 617-266-3619

AREA OF INVESTMENT REGION CONSIDERED: UNITED STATES

MOST DESIRED INVESTMENTS IN FIELDS OF: OPEN TO MANY INVESTMENTS. HIGH TECHNOLOGY, COMPUTER PRODUCTS, BIOTECHNOLOGY, INFORMATIONAL SERVICES, ELECTRONICS, LIFE SCIENCES, ENVIRONMENTAL, SERVICE COMPANIES, MANUFACTURING, COMMUNICATIONS

POSSIBLE CONSIDERATION FOR INVESTMENT IN: OPEN TO OTHER PROPOSALS IN ESTABLISHED COMPANIES

NO INVESTMENT INTEREST WHATSOEVER IN: START-UP COMPANIES, REAL ESTATE, OIL OR GAS

MINIMUM AND MAXIMUM INVESTMENT DOLLAR AMOUNT: $3,000,000+

ATLAS VENTURE

222 Berkeley St.

Boston, MA 02116

PHONE #: 617-859-9290

FAX #: 617-859-9292

AREA OF INVESTMENT REGION CONSIDERED: UNITED STATES AND EUROPE

MOST DESIRED INVESTMENTS IN FIELDS OF: COMPUTER SOFTWARE, INFORMATION SERVICES, INFORMATION TECHNOLOGY, TELECOMMUNICATIONS, MULTIMEDIA, DATA COMMUNICATIONS

POSSIBLE CONSIDERATION FOR INVESTMENT IN: START-UP COMPANIES IN THESE FIELDS ONLY

NO INVESTMENT INTEREST WHATSOEVER IN: ALL OTHER FIELDS

MINIMUM AND MAXIMUM INVESTMENT DOLLAR AMOUNT: $500,000 to $2,000,000

MDT ADVISERS, INC.

20 Acorn Park

Cambridge, MA 02140

PHONE #: 617-498-6333

FAX #: 617-547-1376

AREA OF INVESTMENT REGION CONSIDERED: NEW ENGLAND REGION

MOST DESIRED INVESTMENTS IN FIELDS OF: OPEN TO MANY INVESTMENTS. HIGH TECHNOLOGY, COMPUTER PRODUCTS, BIOTECHNOLOGY, INFORMATIONAL SERVICES, SERVICE COMPANIES, ELECTRONICS, LIFE SCIENCES, ENVIRONMENTAL, MANUFACTURING, COMMUNICATIONS

POSSIBLE CONSIDERATION FOR INVESTMENT IN: OPEN TO OTHER PROPOSALS

NO INVESTMENT INTEREST WHATSOEVER IN: REAL ESTATE, OIL OR GAS

MINIMUM AND MAXIMUM INVESTMENT DOLLAR AMOUNT: $1,000,000 to $3,000,000

COMDISCO VENTURE GROUP

One Newtone Executive Park

2221 Washington, Suite 302

Newtone Lower Falls, MA 02162

PHONE #: 617-244-6622

FAX #: 617-630-5599

AREA OF INVESTMENT REGION CONSIDERED: UNITED STATES

MOST DESIRED INVESTMENTS IN FIELDS OF: OPEN TO MANY INVESTMENTS. HIGH TECHNOLOGY, COMPUTER PRODUCTS, BIOTECHNOLOGY, INFORMATIONAL SERVICES, SERVICE COMPANIES, ELECTRONICS, LIFE SCIENCES, ENVIRONMENTAL, MANUFACTURING, COMMUNICATIONS

POSSIBLE CONSIDERATION FOR INVESTMENT IN: SOME START-UP COMPANIES, THEY WILL DO DEBT FINANCING

NO INVESTMENT INTEREST WHATSOEVER IN: REAL ESTATE, OIL OR GAS

MINIMUM AND MAXIMUM INVESTMENT DOLLAR AMOUNT: $250,000 + VARIES

APPLIED TECHNOLOGY

One Cranberry Hill

Lexington, MA 02173

PHONE #: 617-862-8622

FAX #: 617-862-8367

AREA OF INVESTMENT REGION CONSIDERED: UNITED STATES

MOST DESIRED INVESTMENTS IN FIELDS OF: START-UP COMPANIES, DATA COMMUNICATIONS, TELECOMMUNICATIONS, DATA PROCESSING, INFORMATION SERVICES AND TECHNOLOGY, MULTIMEDIA, CD ROM

POSSIBLE CONSIDERATION FOR INVESTMENT IN: NO OTHER FIELDS

NO INVESTMENT INTEREST WHATSOEVER IN: ALL OTHER FIELDS

MINIMUM AND MAXIMUM INVESTMENT DOLLAR AMOUNT: $100,000 to $1,000,000

WESTON PRESIDIO CAPITAL

40 William St.

Suite 300

Wellesley, MA 02181

PHONE #: 617-237-4700

FAX #: 617-237-6270

AREA OF INVESTMENT REGION CONSIDERED: UNITED STATES

MOST DESIRED INVESTMENTS IN FIELDS OF: HIGH TECHNOLOGY, BIOTECHNOLOGY, MEDICAL HEALTH CARE PRODUCTS, HEALTH CARE ELECTRONICS, LIFE SCIENCES, MEDICINE

POSSIBLE CONSIDERATION FOR INVESTMENT IN: NO OTHER FIELDS

NO INVESTMENT INTEREST WHATSOEVER IN: ALL OTHER FIELDS

MINIMUM AND MAXIMUM INVESTMENT DOLLAR AMOUNT: $1,000,000+

NORTHWEST VENTURE CAPITAL

40 Williams St.

Suite 305

Wellesley, MA 02181

PHONE #: 617-237-5870

FAX #: 617-237-6270

AREA OF INVESTMENT REGION CONSIDERED: UNITED STATES

MOST DESIRED INVESTMENTS IN FIELDS OF: OPEN TO MANY INVESTMENTS. HIGH TECHNOLOGY, COMPUTER PRODUCTS, INFORMATIONAL SERVICES, SERVICE COMPANIES, ELECTRONICS, LIFE SCIENCES, ENVIRONMENTAL, MANUFACTURING, COMMUNICATIONS

POSSIBLE CONSIDERATION FOR INVESTMENT IN: SOME START-UP COMPANIES

NO INVESTMENT INTEREST WHATSOEVER IN: REAL ESTATE, OIL OR GAS

MINIMUM AND MAXIMUM INVESTMENT DOLLAR AMOUNT: $1,500,000 to $5,000,000

GREYLOCK MANAGEMENT CORP

One Federal St.

Boston, MA 02110-2065

PHONE #: 617-423-5525

FAX #: 617-482-0059

AREA OF INVESTMENT REGION CONSIDERED: UNITED STATES

MOST DESIRED INVESTMENTS IN FIELDS OF: OPEN TO MANY INVESTMENTS, HIGH TECHNOLOGY, BIOTECHNOLOGY, MEDICAL PRODUCTS, MEDICAL HEALTH CARE, MEDICAL ELECTRONICS, LIFE SCIENCES, MEDICINE, ENVIRONMENTAL, COMPUTER HARDWARE, COMPUTER SOFTWARE

POSSIBLE CONSIDERATION FOR INVESTMENT IN: SOME START-UP COMPANIES

NO INVESTMENT INTEREST WHATSOEVER IN: REAL ESTATE, OIL, GAS

MINIMUM AND MAXIMUM INVESTMENT DOLLAR AMOUNT: $1,000,000+

MASSACHUSETTS CAPITAL RESOURCE

420 Boylson St.

5th Floor

Boston, MA 02116-4002

PHONE #: 617-536-3900

FAX #: 617-536-7930

AREA OF INVESTMENT REGION CONSIDERED: MASSACHUSETTS ONLY

MOST DESIRED INVESTMENTS IN FIELDS OF: OPEN TO MANY INVESTMENTS. HIGH TECHNOLOGY, MEDICAL ELECTRONICS, LIFE SCIENCES, MEDICAL HEALTH CARE, ENVIRONMENTAL, BIOTECHNOLOGY, INFORMATIONAL SERVICES, MANUFACTURING, COMMUNICATIONS

POSSIBLE CONSIDERATION FOR INVESTMENT IN: OPEN TO OTHER PROPOSALS

NO INVESTMENT INTEREST WHATSOEVER IN: RETAIL, REAL ESTATE, OIL OR GAS, NO START-UP COMPANIES

MINIMUM AND MAXIMUM INVESTMENT DOLLAR AMOUNT: $250,000 +

HARVARD PRIVATE CORP

600 Atlantic Ave.

Boston, MA 02210-2211

PHONE #: 617-523-4400

FAX #: 617-523-1063

AREA OF INVESTMENT REGION CONSIDERED: UNITED STATES

MOST DESIRED INVESTMENTS IN FIELDS OF: COMPUTERS PRODUCTS, MEDICAL HEALTH CARE, REAL ESTATE, HOTELS, OFFICE BUILDINGS, MULTI-FAMILY

POSSIBLE CONSIDERATION FOR INVESTMENT IN: OPEN TO OTHER INVESTMENTS

NO INVESTMENT INTEREST WHATSOEVER IN: OIL, GAS, MOVIES, ENTERTAINMENT

MINIMUM AND MAXIMUM INVESTMENT DOLLAR AMOUNT: $10,000,000 to $20,000,000

COPLEY VENTURE PARTNERS

600 Atlantic Ave.

13th Floor

Boston, MA 02210-2214

PHONE #: 617-722-6030

FAX #: 617-523-7739

AREA OF INVESTMENT REGION CONSIDERED: UNITED STATES

MOST DESIRED INVESTMENTS IN FIELDS OF: HEALTH CARE SERVICES, HEALTH CARE PRODUCTS, ENVIRONMENTAL, BUSINESS AND CONSUMER SERVICES

POSSIBLE CONSIDERATION FOR INVESTMENT IN: NO OTHER FIELDS

NO INVESTMENT INTEREST WHATSOEVER IN: ALL OTHER FIELDS

MINIMUM AND MAXIMUM INVESTMENT DOLLAR AMOUNT: $500,000 to $2,000,000

GROWTH FUNDING LTD

3011 W. Grand Blvd. #321

Detroit, MI 48230-1602

PHONE #: 313-871-3606

FAX #: 313-873-4935

AREA OF INVESTMENT REGION CONSIDERED: MID WEST

MOST DESIRED INVESTMENTS IN FIELDS OF: BIOTECHNOLOGY, LIFE SCIENCES, ENVIRONMENTAL

POSSIBLE CONSIDERATION FOR INVESTMENT IN: NO OTHER FIELDS

NO INVESTMENT INTEREST WHATSOEVER IN: ALL OTHER FIELDS

MINIMUM AND MAXIMUM INVESTMENT DOLLAR AMOUNT: $500,000+

MEDICAL INNOVATION PARTNERS

Opus Center, Suite 421

9900 Bren Rd. E.

Minneapolis, MN 55343

PHONE #: 612-931-0154

FAX #: 612-931-0003

AREA OF INVESTMENT REGION CONSIDERED: UPPER MIDWEST

MOST DESIRED INVESTMENTS IN FIELDS OF: MEDICAL HEALTH CARE PRODUCTS ONLY

POSSIBLE CONSIDERATION FOR INVESTMENT IN: START-UP COMPANIES IN THIS FIELD ONLY

NO INVESTMENT INTEREST WHATSOEVER IN: ALL OTHER FIELDS

MINIMUM AND MAXIMUM INVESTMENT DOLLAR AMOUNT: VARIES

NORTHWEST VENTURE CAPITAL

2800 Piper Jaffray Tower

222 S. 9th St.

Minneapolis, MN 55402

PHONE #: 612-667-1650

FAX #: 612-667-1660

AREA OF INVESTMENT REGION CONSIDERED: UNITED STATES

MOST DESIRED INVESTMENTS IN FIELDS OF: OPEN TO MANY INVESTMENTS. HIGH TECHNOLOGY, COMPUTER PRODUCTS, BIOTECHNOLOGY, INFORMATIONAL SERVICES, SERVICE COMPANIES, ELECTRONICS, LIFE SCIENCES, ENVIRONMENTAL MANUFACTURING, COMMUNICATIONS

POSSIBLE CONSIDERATION FOR INVESTMENT IN: S.B.A. FOR SMALLER LOANS AND WILL WORK WITH START-UP COMPANIES

NO INVESTMENT INTEREST WHATSOEVER IN: REAL ESTATE, OIL OR GAS

MINIMUM AND MAXIMUM INVESTMENT DOLLAR AMOUNT: $1,500,000 to $5,000,000

PIPER JAFFRAY VENTURES, INC.

222 S. 9th St.

13th Floor

Minneapolis, MN 55402

PHONE #: 612-342-6000, Ext. 6310

FAX #: 612-342-6979

AREA OF INVESTMENT REGION CONSIDERED: UNITED STATES

MOST DESIRED INVESTMENTS IN FIELDS OF: ESTABLISHED COMPANIES. HIGH TECHNOLOGY, ELECTRONICS, LIFE SCIENCES, ENVIRONMENTAL, COMPUTER PRODUCTS, BIOTECHNOLOGY, INFORMATIONAL SERVICES, MANUFACTURING, COMMUNICATIONS

POSSIBLE CONSIDERATION FOR INVESTMENT IN: OPEN TO OTHER PROPOSALS

NO INVESTMENT INTEREST WHATSOEVER IN: REAL ESTATE, OIL OR GAS

MINIMUM AND MAXIMUM INVESTMENT DOLLAR AMOUNT: $500,000 to $5,000,000

OAK INVESTMENT PARTNERS

4550 Norwest Center

90 S. 7th St.

Minneapolis, MN 55402

PHONE #: 612-339-9322

FAX #: 612-337-8017

AREA OF INVESTMENT REGION CONSIDERED: UNITED STATES

MOST DESIRED INVESTMENTS IN FIELDS OF: MEDICAL HEALTH CARE PRODUCTS AND SERVICES, SPECIALITY RETAILING, GENERAL HEALTH CARE

POSSIBLE CONSIDERATION FOR INVESTMENT IN: NO OTHER FIELDS

NO INVESTMENT INTEREST WHATSOEVER IN: ALL OTHER FIELDS

MINIMUM AND MAXIMUM INVESTMENT DOLLAR AMOUNT: $2,000,000+

CAPITAL FOR BUSINESS, INC.

11 S. Meramac

Suite 1430

Saint Louis, MO 63105

PHONE #: 314-854-7427

FAX #: 314-746-8739

AREA OF INVESTMENT REGION CONSIDERED: MIDWEST

MOST DESIRED INVESTMENTS IN FIELDS OF: LATER STAGE COMPANIES ONLY. CONSUMER PRODUCTS, MANUFACTURING, MUST HAVE OPERATING REVENUES OF OVER $5,000,000 FOR THEM TO INVEST

POSSIBLE CONSIDERATION FOR INVESTMENT IN: NO OTHERS

NO INVESTMENT INTEREST WHATSOEVER IN: ALL OTHERS

MINIMUM AND MAXIMUM INVESTMENT DOLLAR AMOUNT: $500,000 to $5,000,000

HEARTLAND CAPITAL FUND, LTD.

N.B.C. Center

1248 O St. Suite 880

Lincoln, NB 68508

PHONE #: 402-475-5109

FAX #: 402-475-5170

AREA OF INVESTMENT REGION CONSIDERED: MID AND WESTERN UNITED STATES

MOST DESIRED INVESTMENTS IN FIELDS OF: HIGH TECHNOLOGY, COMPUTER PRODUCTS, ELECTRONICS, ENVIRONMENTAL, TELECOMMUNICATIONS

POSSIBLE CONSIDERATION FOR INVESTMENT IN: SOME START-UP COMPANIES

NO INVESTMENT INTEREST WHATSOEVER IN: ALL OTHER FIELDS

MINIMUM AND MAXIMUM INVESTMENT DOLLAR AMOUNT: $250,000 to 1,000,000

GEOCAPITAL PARTNERS

One Bridge Plaza

Fort Lee, NJ 07024

PHONE #: 201-461-9292

FAX #: 201-346-9191

AREA OF INVESTMENT REGION CONSIDERED: UNITED STATES

MOST DESIRED INVESTMENTS IN FIELDS OF: COMPUTER SOFTWARE, INFORMATIONAL SYSTEMS, DATA COMMUNICATIONS, MULTIMEDIA, INFORMATION TECHNOLOGY

POSSIBLE CONSIDERATION FOR INVESTMENT IN: NO OTHER FIELDS

NO INVESTMENT INTEREST WHATSOEVER IN: ALL OTHER FIELDS

MINIMUM AND MAXIMUM INVESTMENT DOLLAR AMOUNT: $1,000,000+

EDELSON TECHNOLOGY PARTNERS

300 Tice Blvd.

Woodcliff, NJ 07675

PHONE #: 201-930-9898

FAX #: 201-843-5479

AREA OF INVESTMENT REGION CONSIDERED: UNITED STATES

MOST DESIRED INVESTMENTS IN FIELDS OF: NEW TECHNOLOGY PRODUCTS, ELECTRONICS, COMPUTER PRODUCTS, INFORMATION SERVICES, TELECOMMUNICATIONS

POSSIBLE CONSIDERATION FOR INVESTMENT IN: SOME START-UP COMPANIES, IN THESE FIELDS

NO INVESTMENT INTEREST WHATSOEVER IN: ALL OTHER FIELDS

MINIMUM AND MAXIMUM INVESTMENT DOLLAR AMOUNT: $200,000 to $1,000,000

THE VERTICAL GROUP

18 Bank St.

Summit, NJ 07901

PHONE #: 908-277-3737

FAX #: 908-273-9434

AREA OF INVESTMENT REGION CONSIDERED: UNITED STATES

MOST DESIRED INVESTMENTS IN FIELDS OF: MEDICAL HEALTH CARE SERVICES, MEDICAL HEALTH CARE PRODUCTS, BIOTECHNOLOGY, LIFE SCIENCES

POSSIBLE CONSIDERATION FOR INVESTMENT IN: SOME START-UP COMPANIES

NO INVESTMENT INTEREST WHATSOEVER IN: ALL OTHER FIELDS

MINIMUM AND MAXIMUM INVESTMENT DOLLAR AMOUNT: $500,000+

JOHNSTON ASSOCIATES INC.

181 Cherry Valley Rd.

Princeton, NJ 08540

PHONE #: 609-924-3131

FAX #: 609-683-7524

AREA OF INVESTMENT REGION CONSIDERED: UNITED STATES

MOST DESIRED INVESTMENTS IN FIELDS OF: MEDICAL HEALTH CARE PRODUCTS

POSSIBLE CONSIDERATION FOR INVESTMENT IN: SOME START-UP COMPANIES, OPEN TO OTHER PROPOSALS IN MEDICAL FIELDS ONLY

NO INVESTMENT INTEREST WHATSOEVER IN: ALL OTHER FIELDS

MINIMUM AND MAXIMUM INVESTMENT DOLLAR AMOUNT: $250,000 to $2,000,000

DOMAIN ASSOCIATES

One Palmer Square

Suite 515

Princeton, NJ 08542

PHONE #: 609-683-5656

FAX #: 609-683-9789

AREA OF INVESTMENT REGION CONSIDERED: UNITED STATES

MOST DESIRED INVESTMENTS IN FIELDS OF: BIOTECHNOLOGY, MEDICAL HEALTH CARE PRODUCTS, MEDICAL HEALTH SERVICES, MEDICAL ELECTRONICS, LIFE SCIENCES

POSSIBLE CONSIDERATION FOR INVESTMENT IN: SOME START-UP COMPANIES IN THIS FIELD ONLY

NO INVESTMENT INTEREST WHATSOEVER IN: ALL OTHER FIELDS

MINIMUM AND MAXIMUM INVESTMENT DOLLAR AMOUNT: $500,000 to $2,000,000

ACCEL PARTNERS

One Palmer Square

Princeton, NJ 08542

PHONE #: 609-683-4500

FAX #: 609-683-0384

AREA OF INVESTMENT REGION CONSIDERED: UNITED STATES

MOST DESIRED INVESTMENTS IN FIELDS OF: HIGH TECHNOLOGY, ELECTRONICS, LIFE SCIENCES, ENVIRONMENTAL, MEDICAL HEALTH CARE SERVICES, COMPUTER SOFTWARE, TELECOMMUNICATIONS, HEALTH CARE PRODUCTS

POSSIBLE CONSIDERATION FOR INVESTMENT IN: NO OTHER FIELDS

NO INVESTMENT INTEREST WHATSOEVER IN: ALL OTHER FIELDS

MINIMUM AND MAXIMUM INVESTMENT DOLLAR AMOUNT: $1,000,000 to $6,000,000.

DSV PARTNERS

221 Nassau St.

Princeton, NJ 08542

PHONE #: 609-924-6420

FAX #: 609-683-0174

AREA OF INVESTMENT REGION CONSIDERED: UNITED STATES

MOST DESIRED INVESTMENTS IN FIELDS OF: CHEMICALS, COMPUTER SOFTWARE, BIOTECHNOLOGY- ONLY

POSSIBLE CONSIDERATION FOR INVESTMENT IN: NO OTHER FIELDS

NO INVESTMENT INTEREST WHATSOEVER IN: ALL OTHER FIELDS

MINIMUM AND MAXIMUM INVESTMENT DOLLAR AMOUNT: $1,000,000 to $5,000,000

EDISON VENTURE FUND

997 Lenox Drive #3

Lawrenceville, NJ 08648

PHONE #: 609-896-1900

FAX #: 609-896-0066

AREA OF INVESTMENT REGION CONSIDERED: UNITED STATES

MOST DESIRED INVESTMENTS IN FIELDS OF: OPEN TO MANY INVESTMENTS, COMPUTER SOFTWARE, TELECOMMUNICATIONS, HIGH TECHNOLOGY, BIOTECHNOLOGY, INFORMATIONAL SERVICES, ELECTRONICS, LIFE SCIENCES, ENVIRONMENTAL, COMMUNICATIONS

POSSIBLE CONSIDERATION FOR INVESTMENT IN: SOME START-UP COMPANIES, OPEN TO OTHER PROPOSALS

NO INVESTMENT INTEREST WHATSOEVER IN: REAL ESTATE, OIL OR GAS

MINIMUM AND MAXIMUM INVESTMENT DOLLAR AMOUNT: $1,000,000 to $5,000,000

HEALTH CARE INVESTMENTS CORP.

379 Thornall St.

Edison, NJ 08837

PHONE #: 908-906-4600

FAX #: 908-906-1450

AREA OF INVESTMENT REGION CONSIDERED: UNITED STATES

MOST DESIRED INVESTMENTS IN FIELDS OF: MEDICAL HEALTH CARE PRODUCTS AND MEDICAL HEALTH CARE SERVICES INDUSTRY ONLY

POSSIBLE CONSIDERATION FOR INVESTMENT IN: NO OTHER FIELDS

NO INVESTMENT INTEREST WHATSOEVER IN: ALL OTHER FIELDS

MINIMUM AND MAXIMUM INVESTMENT DOLLAR AMOUNT: $1,000,000+

ARGENTUM CAPITAL PARTNERS, L.P.

405 Lexington Ave.

54th Floor

New York, NY 10174

PHONE #: 212-949-6262

FAX #: 212-949-8294

AREA OF INVESTMENT REGION CONSIDERED: EASTERN UNITED STATES

MOST DESIRED INVESTMENTS IN FIELDS OF: MEDICAL PRODUCTS, HEALTH CARE PRODUCTS AND SERVICES, BIOTECHNOLOGY, ENVIRONMENTAL, LIFE SCIENCES

POSSIBLE CONSIDERATION FOR INVESTMENT IN: NO OTHER FIELDS

NO INVESTMENT INTEREST WHATSOEVER IN: ALL OTHER FIELDS

MINIMUM AND MAXIMUM INVESTMENT DOLLAR AMOUNT: $1,000,000+

THE VERTICAL GROUP

61 Broadway

Suite 918

New York, NY 10006

PHONE #: 212-480-0600

FAX #: 212-480-0623

AREA OF INVESTMENT REGION CONSIDERED: UNITED STATES

MOST DESIRED INVESTMENTS IN FIELDS OF: MEDICAL HEALTH CARE SERVICES, MEDICAL HEALTH CARE PRODUCTS, BIOTECHNOLOGY, LIFE SCIENCES

POSSIBLE CONSIDERATION FOR INVESTMENT IN: SOME START-UP COMPANIES IN THESE FIELDS ONLY

NO INVESTMENT INTEREST WHATSOEVER IN: ALL OTHER FIELDS

MINIMUM AND MAXIMUM INVESTMENT DOLLAR AMOUNT: $500,000+

N. Y. LIFE VENTURE CAPITAL GROUP

51 Madison Ave.

Room 206

New York, NY 10010

PHONE #: 212-576-7000, Ext. 6777

FAX #: 212-447-4165

AREA OF INVESTMENT REGION CONSIDERED: UNITED STATES

MOST DESIRED INVESTMENTS IN FIELDS OF: ESTABLISHED COMPANIES, HIGH TECHNOLOGY, COMPUTER SOFTWARE, BIO-TECHNOLOGY, INFORMATIONAL SERVICES, ELECTRONICS, LIFE SCIENCES, ENVIRONMENTAL, COMMUNICATIONS

POSSIBLE CONSIDERATION FOR INVESTMENT IN: ESTABLISHED COMPANIES WITH GROWTH POTENTIAL

NO INVESTMENT INTEREST WHATSOEVER IN: ALL OTHER FIELDS

MINIMUM AND MAXIMUM INVESTMENT DOLLAR AMOUNT: $1,000,000+

ENDEAVOR CAPITAL MANAGEMENT

2 Tudor City Place

Suite 2GN

New York, NY 10017

PHONE #: 212-490-6975

FAX #: 212-490-8549

AREA OF INVESTMENT REGION CONSIDERED: UNITED STATES

MOST DESIRED INVESTMENTS IN FIELDS OF: ESTABLISHED COMPANIES, HIGH TECHNOLOGY, COMPUTER SOFTWARE, INFORMATIONAL SERVICES, ELECTRONICS, COMMUNICATIONS, TELECOMMUNICATIONS

POSSIBLE CONSIDERATION FOR INVESTMENT IN: OTHER ESTABLISHED PRODUCT COMPANIES WITH GROWTH POTENTIAL

NO INVESTMENT INTEREST WHATSOEVER IN: ALL OTHER FIELDS

MINIMUM AND MAXIMUM INVESTMENT DOLLAR AMOUNT: $500,000 to $1,500,000

HARVEST VENTURES, INC.

767 3rd Ave.

New York, NY 10017

PHONE #: 212-838-7776

FAX #: 212-593-0734

AREA OF INVESTMENT REGION CONSIDERED: UNITED STATES

MOST DESIRED INVESTMENTS IN FIELDS OF: ONLY WORKING WITH BUYOUTS

POSSIBLE CONSIDERATION FOR INVESTMENT IN: LOOKING FOR LARGER DEALS

NO INVESTMENT INTEREST WHATSOEVER IN: START-UP COMPANIES, REAL ESTATE, OIL OR GAS

MINIMUM AND MAXIMUM INVESTMENT DOLLAR AMOUNT: $5,000,000+

CAPITAL CITIES CAPITAL, INC.

77 W. 66th Street

New York, NY 10023

PHONE #: 212-456-7224

FAX #: 212-456-3928

AREA OF INVESTMENT REGION CONSIDERED: UNITED STATES

MOST DESIRED INVESTMENTS IN FIELDS OF: ESTABLISHED CONSUMER PRODUCT COMPANIES

IMPORTANT: THEY HELP WITH ADVERTISING AND DISTRIBUTION OF YOUR COMPANIES' CONSUMER PRODUCTS. THEY WILL ADVERTISE AND DISTRIBUTE FOR AN EQUITY OWNERSHIP IN YOUR COMPANY. *THEY WILL NOT INVEST CAPITAL INTO THE COMPANY.*

POSSIBLE CONSIDERATION FOR INVESTMENT IN: NO OTHER COMPANIES OR FIELDS

NO INVESTMENT INTEREST WHATSOEVER IN: NO START-UPS OR EARLY STAGE COMPANIES

MINIMUM AND MAXIMUM INVESTMENT DOLLAR AMOUNT: VARIES

NORWOOD VENTURE CORP

1430 Broadway

Suite 1607

New York, NY 10018

PHONE #: 212-869-5075

FAX #: 212-869-5331

AREA OF INVESTMENT REGION CONSIDERED: UNITED STATES

MOST DESIRED INVESTMENTS IN FIELDS OF: LOW TECHNOLOGY, INFORMATIONAL SERVICES, MANUFACTURING, COMMUNICATIONS

POSSIBLE CONSIDERATION FOR INVESTMENT IN: ESTABLISHED COMPANIES ONLY

NO INVESTMENT INTEREST WHATSOEVER IN: ALL OTHER FIELDS

MINIMUM AND MAXIMUM INVESTMENT DOLLAR AMOUNT: $200,000 to $1,000,000

ROTHSCHILD VENTURES INC

VENTURE CAPITAL GROUP

1251 Avenue of Americas

New York, NY 10020

PHONE #: 212-757-6000 OR 212-403-3636

FAX #: 212-403-3501

AREA OF INVESTMENT REGION CONSIDERED: UNITED STATES

MOST DESIRED INVESTMENTS IN FIELDS OF: HIGH TECHNOLOGY, MATERIAL SCIENCES, BIOTECHNOLOGY

POSSIBLE CONSIDERATION FOR INVESTMENT IN: NO OTHER FIELDS

NO INVESTMENT INTEREST WHATSOEVER IN: ALL OTHER FIELDS

MINIMUM AND MAXIMUM INVESTMENT DOLLAR AMOUNT: $500,000 to $2,000,000+

CW GROUP

1041 Third Ave.

New York, NY 10021

PHONE #: 212-308-5266

FAX #: 212-644-0354

AREA OF INVESTMENT REGION CONSIDERED: UNITED STATES

MOST DESIRED INVESTMENTS IN FIELDS OF: MEDICAL HEALTH CARE PRODUCTS AND MEDICAL HEALTH CARE SERVICES, BIO-TECHNOLOGY MEDICAL FIELDS

POSSIBLE CONSIDERATION FOR INVESTMENT IN: NO OTHER FIELDS

NO INVESTMENT INTEREST WHATSOEVER IN: ALL OTHER FIELDS

MINIMUM AND MAXIMUM INVESTMENT DOLLAR AMOUNT: $500,000+

THE LAMBDA FUNDS

41 East 57th St.

31st Floor

New York, NY 10022

PHONE #: 212-838-0005

FAX #: 212-838-0144

AREA OF INVESTMENT REGION CONSIDERED: MID ATLANTIC AREA

MOST DESIRED INVESTMENTS IN FIELDS OF: HIGH TECHNOLOGY, COMPUTER PRODUCTS, ELECTRONICS, LIFE SCIENCES, ENVIRONMENTAL, BIOTECHNOLOGY, MEDICAL HEALTH CARE PRODUCTS

POSSIBLE CONSIDERATION FOR INVESTMENT IN: SOME START-UP COMPANIES, OPEN TO OTHER PROPOSALS

NO INVESTMENT INTEREST WHATSOEVER IN: REAL ESTATE, OIL OR GAS

MINIMUM AND MAXIMUM INVESTMENT DOLLAR AMOUNT: $1,000,000 +

INTERNATIONAL TECHNOLOGY VENTURES, INC.

70 E. 55th St.
24th Floor
New York, NY 10022
PHONE #: 212-972-5235
FAX #: 212-319-8965

AREA OF INVESTMENT REGION CONSIDERED: UNITED STATES

MOST DESIRED INVESTMENTS IN FIELDS OF: OPEN TO MANY INVESTMENTS. HIGH TECHNOLOGY, COMPUTER PRODUCTS, BIOTECHNOLOGY, INFORMATIONAL SERVICES, SERVICE COMPANIES, ELECTRONICS, LIFE SCIENCES, ENVIRONMENTAL, MANUFACTURING, COMMUNICATIONS

POSSIBLE CONSIDERATION FOR INVESTMENT IN: OPEN TO OTHER PROPOSALS

NO INVESTMENT INTEREST WHATSOEVER IN: REAL ESTATE, OIL OR GAS

MINIMUM AND MAXIMUM INVESTMENT DOLLAR AMOUNT: $500,000 VARIES, CASE BY CASE

HAMBRO INTERNATIONAL EQUITY PARTNERS

650 Madison Ave.

21st Floor

New York, NY 10022

PHONE #: 212-223-7400

FAX #: 212-223-0305

AREA OF INVESTMENT REGION CONSIDERED: UNITED STATES

MOST DESIRED INVESTMENTS IN FIELDS OF: OPEN TO MANY INVESTMENTS. HIGH TECHNOLOGY, COMPUTER PRODUCTS, BIOTECHNOLOGY, INFORMATIONAL SERVICES, SERVICE COMPANIES, ELECTRONICS, LIFE SCIENCES, ENVIRONMENTAL, MANUFACTURING, COMMUNICATIONS

POSSIBLE CONSIDERATION FOR INVESTMENT IN: OPEN TO OTHER PROPOSALS

NO INVESTMENT INTEREST WHATSOEVER IN: REAL ESTATE, OIL OR GAS

MINIMUM AND MAXIMUM INVESTMENT DOLLAR AMOUNT: $2,000,000 to $5,000,000

MCCOWN DE LEEUW & CO.

900 Third Ave.

28th Floor

New York, NY 10022

PHONE #: 212-355-5500

FAX #: 212-418-6584

AREA OF INVESTMENT REGION CONSIDERED: UNITED STATES

MOST DESIRED INVESTMENTS IN FIELDS OF: OPEN TO MANY INVESTMENTS. HIGH TECHNOLOGY, COMPUTER PRODUCTS, BIOTECHNOLOGY, INFORMATIONAL SERVICES, SERVICE COMPANIES, ELECTRONICS, LIFE SCIENCES, ENVIRONMENTAL, MANUFACTURING, COMMUNICATIONS

POSSIBLE CONSIDERATION FOR INVESTMENT IN: OPEN TO OTHER PROPOSALS

NO INVESTMENT INTEREST WHATSOEVER IN: REAL ESTATE, OIL OR GAS

MINIMUM AND MAXIMUM INVESTMENT DOLLAR AMOUNT: MINIMUM AMOUNT GREATER THAN $20,000,000+

NORTHWOOD VENTURES

485 Underhill Blvd.

Suite 205

Syosset, NY 11791

PHONE #: 516-364-5544

FAX #: 516-364-0879

AREA OF INVESTMENT REGION CONSIDERED: UNITED STATES

MOST DESIRED INVESTMENTS IN FIELDS OF: OPEN TO MANY INVESTMENTS. HIGH TECHNOLOGY, COMPUTER PRODUCTS, BIOTECHNOLOGY, INFORMATIONAL SERVICES, ELECTRONICS, LIFE SCIENCES, ENVIRONMENTAL, SERVICE COMPANIES, MANUFACTURING, COMMUNICATIONS

POSSIBLE CONSIDERATION FOR INVESTMENT IN: OPEN TO OTHER PROPOSALS

NO INVESTMENT INTEREST WHATSOEVER IN: REAL ESTATE, OIL OR GAS

MINIMUM AND MAXIMUM INVESTMENT DOLLAR AMOUNT: $1,000,000+

BRADFORD VENTURES LTD.

1212 Avenue of the Americas

New York, NY 10036

PHONE #: 212-221-4620

FAX #: 212-764-3467

AREA OF INVESTMENT REGION CONSIDERED: MIDWEST AND NORTHEAST UNITED STATES

MOST DESIRED INVESTMENTS IN FIELDS OF: ESTABLISH COMPANIES IN, MANUFACTURING, DISTRIBUTION, SERVICE COMPANIES, LOW TECHNOLOGY

POSSIBLE CONSIDERATION FOR INVESTMENT IN: NO OTHER FIELDS

NO INVESTMENT INTEREST WHATSOEVER IN: ALL OTHER FIELDS

MINIMUM AND MAXIMUM INVESTMENT DOLLAR AMOUNT: $5,000,000 to $10,000,000

CITICORP VENTURE CAPITAL, LTD.

399 Park Ave.

New York, NY 10043

PHONE #: 212-559-1127

FAX #: 212-888-2940

AREA OF INVESTMENT REGION CONSIDERED: UNITED STATES

MOST DESIRED INVESTMENTS IN FIELDS OF: COMPANIES MUST BE OVER 5 YEARS OLD. OPEN TO MANY INVESTMENTS, ALSO LOOKING FOR LEVERAGED BUYOUTS

POSSIBLE CONSIDERATION FOR INVESTMENT IN: OPEN TO OTHER PROPOSALS

NO INVESTMENT INTEREST WHATSOEVER IN: REAL ESTATE, OIL OR GAS

MINIMUM AND MAXIMUM INVESTMENT DOLLAR AMOUNT: $1,000,000 to $10,000,000+

CHASE MANHATTAN CAPITAL CORP

One Chase Manhattan Plaza.

8th Floor

New York, NY 10081

PHONE #: 212-552-1347

FAX #: 212-552-1159

AREA OF INVESTMENT REGION CONSIDERED: UNITED STATES

MOST DESIRED INVESTMENTS IN FIELDS OF: OPEN TO MANY INVESTMENTS. HIGH TECHNOLOGY, COMPUTER PRODUCTS, BIOTECHNOLOGY, ELECTRONICS, LIFE SCIENCES, ENVIRONMENTAL, INFORMATIONAL SERVICES, SERVICE COMPANIES, MANUFACTURING, COMMUNICATIONS

POSSIBLE CONSIDERATION FOR INVESTMENT IN: SOME START-UP COMPANIES, OPEN TO OTHER PROPOSALS

NO INVESTMENT INTEREST WHATSOEVER IN: REAL ESTATE, OIL OR GAS

MINIMUM AND MAXIMUM INVESTMENT DOLLAR AMOUNT: $1,000,000 +

VENROCK ASSOCIATES

30 Rockefeller Plaza

Room 5508

New York, NY 10112

PHONE #: 212-649-5600

FAX #: 212-649-5788

AREA OF INVESTMENT REGION CONSIDERED: UNITED STATES

MOST DESIRED INVESTMENTS IN FIELDS OF: LEADING EDGE TECHNOLOGY COMPANIES ONLY. HIGH TECHNOLOGY, BIO-TECHNOLOGY, ROBOTICS, MEDICAL HEALTH CARE PRODUCTS, COMPUTERS PRODUCTS, MATERIAL SCIENCE, COMMUNICATIONS, TELE-COMMUNICATIONS

POSSIBLE CONSIDERATION FOR INVESTMENT IN: NO OTHER FIELDS

NO INVESTMENT INTEREST WHATSOEVER IN: ALL OTHER FIELDS

MINIMUM AND MAXIMUM INVESTMENT DOLLAR AMOUNT: $500,000 to $2,000,000

JP MORGAN CAPITAL CORP.

60 Wall St.

New York, NY 10260

PHONE #: 212-648-9781

FAX #: 212-648-5032

AREA OF INVESTMENT REGION CONSIDERED: UNITED STATES

MOST DESIRED INVESTMENTS IN FIELDS OF: OPEN TO MANY INVESTMENTS. HIGH TECHNOLOGY, COMPUTER PRODUCTS, BIOTECHNOLOGY, ELECTRONICS, LIFE SCIENCES, ENVIRONMENTAL, INFORMATIONAL SERVICES, SERVICE COMPANIES, MANUFACTURING, COMMUNICATIONS

POSSIBLE CONSIDERATION FOR INVESTMENT IN: OPEN TO OTHER PROPOSALS IN THESE FIELDS

NO INVESTMENT INTEREST WHATSOEVER IN: ALL OTHER FIELDS

MINIMUM AND MAXIMUM INVESTMENT DOLLAR AMOUNT: MINIMUM OF $10,000,000+

VENTURE OPPORTUNITIES CORP.

150 E. 58th Street

New York, NY 10155

PHONE #: 212-832-3737

FAX #: 212-980-6603

AREA OF INVESTMENT REGION CONSIDERED: EASTERN UNITED STATES. MAY CONSIDER ALL OF UNITED STATES

MOST DESIRED INVESTMENTS IN FIELDS OF: WILL LOOK AT ANY MINORITY-OWNED BUSINESS. THE BUSINESS MUST BE OVER 51% MINORITY OWNED TO BE CONSIDERED FOR FUNDING.

POSSIBLE CONSIDERATION FOR INVESTMENT IN: IN MANY AREAS

NO INVESTMENT INTEREST WHATSOEVER IN: REAL ESTATE, OIL OR GAS

MINIMUM AND MAXIMUM INVESTMENT DOLLAR AMOUNT: $100,000 + VARIES

LAWRENCE, SMITH & HOREY

515 Madison Ave.

29th Floor

New York, NY 10022-5403

PHONE #: 212-826-9080

FAX #: 212-759-2561

AREA OF INVESTMENT REGION CONSIDERED: EAST COAST

MOST DESIRED INVESTMENTS IN FIELDS OF: COMPUTER SOFTWARE

POSSIBLE CONSIDERATION FOR INVESTMENT IN: NO OTHER FIELDS

NO INVESTMENT INTEREST WHATSOEVER IN: ALL OTHER FIELDS

MINIMUM AND MAXIMUM INVESTMENT DOLLAR AMOUNT: $1,000,000+

PATRICOF & CO. VENTURES, INC.

445 Park Ave.

New York, NY 10022

PHONE #: 212-753-6300

FAX #: 212-391-6155

AREA OF INVESTMENT REGION CONSIDERED: UNITED STATES

MOST DESIRED INVESTMENTS IN FIELDS OF: HEALTH CARE PRODUCTS AND SERVICES, CONSUMER PRODUCTS MANUFACTURING COMPANIES, TELECOMMUNICATIONS, COMPUTER HARDWARE, SOFTWARE

POSSIBLE CONSIDERATION FOR INVESTMENT IN: PREFERS LATER STAGE COMPANIES. BUT WILL LOOK AT EARLY STAGE COMPANIES WITH HIGH GROWTH POTENTIAL.

NO INVESTMENT INTEREST WHATSOEVER IN: ALL OTHER FIELDS

MINIMUM AND MAXIMUM INVESTMENT DOLLAR AMOUNT: $7,000,000+

ATLANTIC VENTURE PARTNERS

380 Knollwood St.
Suite 606
Winston Salem, NC 27103
PHONE #: 910-725-2961
FAX #: 910-725-4356

AREA OF INVESTMENT REGION CONSIDERED: UNITED STATES

MOST DESIRED INVESTMENTS IN FIELDS OF: COMPANY MUST HAVE MINIMUM OF $5,000,000 IN REVENUES. HIGH TECHNOLOGY, INFORMATION SERVICES, BIOTECHNOLOGY, MULTIMEDIA, TELECOMMUNICATIONS, ELECTRONICS, LIFE SCIENCES, ENVIRONMENTAL

POSSIBLE CONSIDERATION FOR INVESTMENT IN: OPEN TO OTHER INVESTMENTS

NO INVESTMENT INTEREST WHATSOEVER IN: START-UP COMPANIES OR EARLY STAGE COMPANIES.

MINIMUM AND MAXIMUM INVESTMENT DOLLAR AMOUNT: $1,000,000 to $2,500,000

THE NORTH CAROLINA ENTERPRISE FUND, INC.

3600 Glenwood Ave. Suite 107
Raleigh, NC 27612
PHONE #: 919-781-2691
FAX #: 919-783-9195

AREA OF INVESTMENT REGION CONSIDERED: NORTH CAROLINA

MOST DESIRED INVESTMENTS IN FIELDS OF: OPEN TO MANY INVESTMENTS. HIGH TECHNOLOGY, COMPUTER PRODUCTS, BIOTECHNOLOGY, INFORMATIONAL SERVICES, SERVICE COMPANIES, MANUFACTURING, COMMUNICATIONS, ELECTRONICS, LIFE SCIENCES, ENVIRONMENTAL

POSSIBLE CONSIDERATION FOR INVESTMENT IN: SOME START-UP COMPANIES, OPEN TO OTHER PROPOSALS

NO INVESTMENT INTEREST WHATSOEVER IN: REAL ESTATE, OIL OR GAS

MINIMUM AND MAXIMUM INVESTMENT DOLLAR AMOUNT: $250,000 to $1,500,000

CAROLINAS CAPITAL INVESTMENT CORP

6337 Morrison Blvd.

Charlotte, NC 28211-3510

PHONE #: 704-362-8222

FAX #: 704-362-8221

AREA OF INVESTMENT REGION CONSIDERED: N. & S. CAROLINA, GEORGIA, VIRGINIA

MOST DESIRED INVESTMENTS IN FIELDS OF: ESTABLISHED COMPANIES, MUST HAVE CURRENT SALES. LOW TECHNOLOGY COMPANIES, ONLY

POSSIBLE CONSIDERATION FOR INVESTMENT IN: NO OTHERS

NO INVESTMENT INTEREST WHATSOEVER IN: START-UP COMPANIES

MINIMUM AND MAXIMUM INVESTMENT DOLLAR AMOUNT: $200,000 to $600,000

PIEDMONT VENTURE PARTNERS LLC

1901 Roxborough Rd.

Suite 120

Charlotte, NC 28211

PHONE #: 704-364-5800

FAX #: 704-364-6700

AREA OF INVESTMENT REGION CONSIDERED: N. AND S. CAROLINA

MOST DESIRED INVESTMENTS IN FIELDS OF: OPEN TO MANY INVESTMENTS, HIGH TECHNOLOGY, COMPUTER PRODUCTS, BIOTECHNOLOGY, INFORMATIONAL SERVICES, SERVICE COMPANIES, MANUFACTURING, COMMUNICATIONS, ELECTRONICS, LIFE SCIENCES, ENVIRONMENTAL

POSSIBLE CONSIDERATION FOR INVESTMENT IN: SOME START-UP COMPANIES

NO INVESTMENT INTEREST WHATSOEVER IN: REAL ESTATE OIL AND GAS

MINIMUM AND MAXIMUM INVESTMENT DOLLAR AMOUNT: VARIES

KITTY HAWK CAPITAL

2101 Rexford Rd.

#203-E

Charlotte, NC 28211

PHONE #: 704-362-3909

FAX #: 704-362-2774

AREA OF INVESTMENT REGION CONSIDERED: SOUTHEASTERN U.S. ONLY

MOST DESIRED INVESTMENTS IN FIELDS OF: OPEN TO MANY INVESTMENTS. HIGH TECHNOLOGY, COMPUTER PRODUCTS, BIOTECHNOLOGY, INFORMATIONAL SERVICES, SERVICE COMPANIES, ELECTRONICS, LIFE SCIENCES, ENVIRONMENTAL, MANUFACTURING, COMMUNICATIONS

POSSIBLE CONSIDERATION FOR INVESTMENT IN: SOME START-UP COMPANIES, OPEN TO OTHER PROPOSALS

NO INVESTMENT INTEREST WHATSOEVER IN: REAL ESTATE, OIL OR GAS

MINIMUM AND MAXIMUM INVESTMENT DOLLAR AMOUNT: $500,000 to $2,000,000

NORTHWEST OHIO VENTURE FUND

300 Madison Ave.

Suite 1525

Toledo, OH 43604

PHONE #: 419-244-9112

FAX #: 419-244-9554

AREA OF INVESTMENT REGION CONSIDERED: OHIO & MICHIGAN

MOST DESIRED INVESTMENTS IN FIELDS OF: OPEN TO MANY INVESTMENTS. HIGH TECHNOLOGY, COMPUTER PRODUCTS, BIOTECHNOLOGY, ELECTRONICS, LIFE SCIENCES, ENVIRONMENTAL, INFORMATIONAL SERVICES, SERVICE COMPANIES, MANUFACTURING, COMMUNICATIONS

POSSIBLE CONSIDERATION FOR INVESTMENT IN: OPEN TO OTHER PROPOSALS

NO INVESTMENT INTEREST WHATSOEVER IN: REAL ESTATE, OIL OR GAS

MINIMUM AND MAXIMUM INVESTMENT DOLLAR AMOUNT: $150,000, BUT PREFERS $1,000,000 AND OVER

LUBRIZOL PERFORMANCE PRODUCTS CO.

VENTURE CAPITAL GROUP

Strategic Planning & Investment Div.

29400 Lakeland Blvd.

Wickliffe, OH 44092

PHONE #: 216-943-4200

FAX #: 216-944-8112

AREA OF INVESTMENT REGION CONSIDERED: UNITED STATES

MOST DESIRED INVESTMENTS IN FIELDS OF: SPECIALITY CHEMICALS ONLY

POSSIBLE CONSIDERATION FOR INVESTMENT IN: NO OTHER FIELDS

NO INVESTMENT INTEREST WHATSOEVER IN: ALL OTHER FIELDS

MINIMUM AND MAXIMUM INVESTMENT DOLLAR AMOUNT: VARIES

NEW ENTERPRISE ASSOC.

One Cleveland Center

Suite 2700

Cleveland, OH 44114

PHONE #: 216-861-4800

FAX #: 216-621-4543

AREA OF INVESTMENT REGION CONSIDERED: UNITED STATES

MOST DESIRED INVESTMENTS IN FIELDS OF: SPECIALTY CHEMICAL AND MATERIALS ONLY

POSSIBLE CONSIDERATION FOR INVESTMENT IN: SOME START-UP COMPANIES

NO INVESTMENT INTEREST WHATSOEVER IN: ALL OTHER FIELDS

MINIMUM AND MAXIMUM INVESTMENT DOLLAR AMOUNT: $500,000+

PRIMUS VENTURE PARTNERS

1735 East Ninth St.

Suite 2700

Cleveland, OH 44114

PHONE #: 216-621-2185

FAX #: 216-621-4543

AREA OF INVESTMENT REGION CONSIDERED: UNITED STATES

MOST DESIRED INVESTMENTS IN FIELDS OF: OPEN TO MANY INVESTMENTS. HIGH TECHNOLOGY, COMPUTER PRODUCTS, BIOTECHNOLOGY, INFORMATIONAL SERVICES, ELECTRONICS, LIFE SCIENCES, ENVIRONMENTAL, SERVICE COMPANIES, MANUFACTURING, COMMUNICATIONS

POSSIBLE CONSIDERATION FOR INVESTMENT IN: OPEN TO OTHER PROPOSALS

NO INVESTMENT INTEREST WHATSOEVER IN: REAL ESTATE, OIL OR GAS

MINIMUM AND MAXIMUM INVESTMENT DOLLAR AMOUNT: $2,000,000 to $5,000,000

BRANTLY VENTURE PARTNERS, L.P.

20600 Chagrin Blvd.

Suite 510, Tower E.

Cleveland, OH 44122

PHONE #: 216-283-4800

FAX #: 216-283-5324

AREA OF INVESTMENT REGION CONSIDERED: EASTERN UNITED STATES

MOST DESIRED INVESTMENTS IN FIELDS OF: OPEN TO MANY INVESTMENTS. HIGH TECHNOLOGY, ELECTRONICS, LIFE SCIENCES, ENVIRONMENTAL, COMPUTER PRODUCTS, BIOTECHNOLOGY, INFORMATIONAL SERVICES, SERVICE COMPANIES, MANUFACTURING, COMMUNICATIONS

POSSIBLE CONSIDERATION FOR INVESTMENT IN: SOME START-UP COMPANIES, OPEN TO OTHER PROPOSALS

NO INVESTMENT INTEREST WHATSOEVER IN: REAL ESTATE, OIL OR GAS

MINIMUM AND MAXIMUM INVESTMENT DOLLAR AMOUNT: $500,000 to $1,500,000

KEY EQUITY CAPITAL

127 Public Square

6th Floor

Cleveland, OH 44114-1306

PHONE #: 216-689-5776

FAX #: 216-689-3204

AREA OF INVESTMENT REGION CONSIDERED: UNITED STATES

MOST DESIRED INVESTMENTS IN FIELDS OF: OPEN TO MANY INVESTMENTS. HIGH TECHNOLOGY, COMPUTER PRODUCTS, BIOTECHNOLOGY, INFORMATIONAL SERVICES, SERVICE COMPANIES, ELECTRONICS, LIFE SCIENCES, ENVIRONMENTAL, MANUFACTURING, COMMUNICATIONS

POSSIBLE CONSIDERATION FOR INVESTMENT IN: OPEN TO OTHER PROPOSALS

NO INVESTMENT INTEREST WHATSOEVER IN: REAL ESTATE, OIL OR GAS

MINIMUM AND MAXIMUM INVESTMENT DOLLAR AMOUNT: $1,500,000+

CLARION CAPITAL CORP

1801 E. 9th St.

Suite 510

Cleveland, OH 44114-3103

PHONE #: 216-687-1096

FAX #: 216-694-3545

AREA OF INVESTMENT REGION CONSIDERED: MIDWEST

MOST DESIRED INVESTMENTS IN FIELDS OF: OPEN TO MANY INVESTMENTS IN ESTABLISHED COMPANIES. HIGH TECHNOLOGY, COMPUTER PRODUCTS, BIOTECHNOLOGY, INFORMATIONAL SERVICES, SERVICE COMPANIES, ELECTRONICS, LIFE SCIENCES, ENVIRONMENTAL, MANUFACTURING, COMMUNICATIONS

POSSIBLE CONSIDERATION FOR INVESTMENT IN: OTHER ESTABLISHED COMPANIES

NO INVESTMENT INTEREST WHATSOEVER IN: REAL ESTATE AND ALL OTHER FIELDS

MINIMUM AND MAXIMUM INVESTMENT DOLLAR AMOUNT: $250,000 to $1,000,000

CHISHOLM PRIVATE CAPITAL

5100 E. Skelly Dr.

Suite 1060

Tulsa, OK 74135

PHONE #: 918-663-2500

FAX #: 918-663-1140

AREA OF INVESTMENT REGION CONSIDERED: TEXAS, OK

MOST DESIRED INVESTMENTS IN FIELDS OF: HIGH TECHNOLOGY, MANUFACTURING COMPANIES, ELECTRONICS

POSSIBLE CONSIDERATION FOR INVESTMENT IN: ESTABLISHED COMPANIES, AND SOME START-UP COMPANIES IN THESE FIELDS

NO INVESTMENT INTEREST WHATSOEVER IN: ALL OTHER COMPANIES

MINIMUM AND MAXIMUM INVESTMENT DOLLAR AMOUNT: $1,000,000+

RBC VENTURES INC.

P.O. Box 52586

Tulsa, OK 74152

PHONE #: 918-744-5607

FAX #: 918-743-8630

AREA OF INVESTMENT REGION CONSIDERED: UNITED STATES

MOST DESIRED INVESTMENTS IN FIELDS OF: MID STAGE AND ESTABLISHED COMPANIES. OPEN TO MANY INVESTMENTS. HIGH TECHNOLOGY, COMPUTER PRODUCTS, BIOTECHNOLOGY, INFORMATIONAL SERVICES, SERVICE COMPANIES, ELECTRONICS, LIFE SCIENCES, ENVIRONMENTAL, MANUFACTURING, COMMUNICATIONS

POSSIBLE CONSIDERATION FOR INVESTMENT IN: UNPROFITABLE COMPANIES IN THESE FIELDS

NO INVESTMENT INTEREST WHATSOEVER IN: START-UP COMPANIES

MINIMUM AND MAXIMUM INVESTMENT DOLLAR AMOUNT: $500,000 +

DAVIS VENTURE PARTNERS

One Williams Center

Suite 2000

Tulsa, OK 74172

PHONE #: 918-584-7272

FAX #: 918-582-3403

AREA OF INVESTMENT REGION CONSIDERED: SOUTH WEST & SOUTH CENTRAL US.

MOST DESIRED INVESTMENTS IN FIELDS OF: OPEN TO MANY INVESTMENTS. HIGH TECHNOLOGY, COMPUTER PRODUCTS, BIOTECHNOLOGY, INFORMATIONAL SERVICES, SERVICE COMPANIES, ELECTRONICS, LIFE SCIENCES, ENVIRONMENTAL, MANUFACTURING, COMMUNICATIONS

POSSIBLE CONSIDERATION FOR INVESTMENT IN: SOME START-UP COMPANIES, OPEN TO OTHER PROPOSALS

NO INVESTMENT INTEREST WHATSOEVER IN: REAL ESTATE, OIL OR GAS

MINIMUM AND MAXIMUM INVESTMENT DOLLAR AMOUNT: $1,000,000 to $10,000,000+

OLYMPIC VENTURE PARTNERS

340 Oswego Point Dr.

Suite 204

Lake Oswego, OR 97034

PHONE #: 503-697-8766

FAX #: 503-697-8863

AREA OF INVESTMENT REGION CONSIDERED: WESTERN U.S.

MOST DESIRED INVESTMENTS IN FIELDS OF: HIGH TECHNOLOGY, MEDICAL HEALTH CARE PRODUCTS, MEDICAL ELECTRONICS, LIFE SCIENCES, MEDICAL HEALTH CARE SERVICES

POSSIBLE CONSIDERATION FOR INVESTMENT IN: PREFERS START-UP COMPANIES IN THESE FIELDS ONLY

NO INVESTMENT INTEREST WHATSOEVER IN: ALL OTHER FIELDS

MINIMUM AND MAXIMUM INVESTMENT DOLLAR AMOUNT: $100,000 to $1,500,000

PNC VENTURE CAPITAL GROUP

5th Ave. & Wood St.

Pittsburgh, PA 15222

PHONE #: 412-762-8892

FAX #: 412-762-6233

AREA OF INVESTMENT REGION CONSIDERED: MIDWEST AND NORTHWEST

MOST DESIRED INVESTMENTS IN FIELDS OF: OPEN TO MANY INVESTMENTS IN ESTABLISHED COMPANIES. HIGH TECHNOLOGY, COMPUTER PRODUCTS, BIOTECHNOLOGY, INFORMATIONAL SERVICES, SERVICE COMPANIES, ELECTRONICS, LIFE SCIENCES, ENVIRONMENTAL, MANUFACTURING, COMMUNICATIONS

POSSIBLE CONSIDERATION FOR INVESTMENT IN: OTHER ESTABLISHED COMPANIES IN THESE FIELDS

NO INVESTMENT INTEREST WHATSOEVER IN: START-UP COMPANIES, REAL ESTATE, OIL, GAS

MINIMUM AND MAXIMUM INVESTMENT DOLLAR AMOUNT: $2,000,000 to $7,000,000

PENNSYLVANIA GROWTH FUND

5850 Ellsworth Ave.

Suite 303

Pittsburgh, PA 15232

PHONE #: 412-361-0500

FAX #: 412-361-0676

AREA OF INVESTMENT REGION CONSIDERED: WESTERN PA. AND SURROUNDING PENNSYLVANIA AREA ONLY

MOST DESIRED INVESTMENTS IN FIELDS OF: ESTABLISHED COMPANIES WITH NEW GROWTH POTENTIAL

POSSIBLE CONSIDERATION FOR INVESTMENT IN: NO OTHER FIELDS

NO INVESTMENT INTEREST WHATSOEVER IN: START-UP COMPANIES, HIGH TECHNOLOGY TYPE COMPANIES

MINIMUM AND MAXIMUM INVESTMENT DOLLAR AMOUNT: $500,000 to $2,000,000

HILLMAN MEDICAL VENTURES, INC.

Two Walnut Grove Dr.

Suite #130

Horsham, PA 19044

PHONE #: 215-443-5531

FAX #: 215-443-5970

AREA OF INVESTMENT REGION CONSIDERED: EAST COAST

MOST DESIRED INVESTMENTS IN FIELDS OF: ALL MEDICAL HEALTH CARE PRODUCTS, MEDICAL HEALTH CARE SERVICES

POSSIBLE CONSIDERATION FOR INVESTMENT IN: START-UP COMPANIES, RESEARCH AND DEVELOPMENT PROJECTS

NO INVESTMENT INTEREST WHATSOEVER IN: ALL OTHER FIELDS

MINIMUM AND MAXIMUM INVESTMENT DOLLAR AMOUNT: $500,000+

PHILADELPHIA VENTURES

200 S. Broad St.

Philadelphia, PA 19102

PHONE #: 215-732-4445

FAX #: 215-732-4644

AREA OF INVESTMENT REGION CONSIDERED: UNITED STATES

MOST DESIRED INVESTMENTS IN FIELDS OF: HIGH TECHNOLOGY, BIOTECHNOLOGY, TELECOMMUNICATIONS, COMPUTER HARDWARE, INFORMATIONAL SERVICES, SERVICE COMPANIES, ELECTRONICS, LIFE SCIENCES, COMPUTER COMMUNICATIONS AND SOFTWARE

POSSIBLE CONSIDERATION FOR INVESTMENT IN: NO OTHER FIELDS

NO INVESTMENT INTEREST WHATSOEVER IN: ALL OTHER FIELDS

MINIMUM AND MAXIMUM INVESTMENT DOLLAR AMOUNT: $500,000+

MERIDIAN VENTURE PARTNERS

The Fidelity Court Building

Suite 140

259 Radnor Chester Rd.

Radnor, PA 19087

PHONE #: 610-254-2999

FAX #: 610-254-2996

AREA OF INVESTMENT REGION CONSIDERED: MID ATLANTIC

MOST DESIRED INVESTMENTS IN FIELDS OF: OPEN TO MANY INVESTMENTS. HIGH TECHNOLOGY, INFORMATIONAL SERVICES, MANUFACTURING, COMMUNICATIONS, ELECTRONICS

POSSIBLE CONSIDERATION FOR INVESTMENT IN: ESTABLISHED COMPANIES. NO START-UP COMPANIES

NO INVESTMENT INTEREST WHATSOEVER IN: REAL ESTATE, OIL OR GAS

MINIMUM AND MAXIMUM INVESTMENT DOLLAR AMOUNT: $1,000,000+

GREATER PHILADELPHIA VENTURE CAPITAL CORP.

351 E. Conestoga Rd.

Wayne, PA 19087-2508

PHONE #: 610-688-6829

FAX #: 610-254-8958

AREA OF INVESTMENT REGION CONSIDERED: PHILADELPHIA AREA ONLY

MOST DESIRED INVESTMENTS IN FIELDS OF: OPEN TO MANY INVESTMENTS FOR MINORITIES ONLY

POSSIBLE CONSIDERATION FOR INVESTMENT IN: SOME START-UP COMPANIES, S.B.A. LOANS AVAILABLE

NO INVESTMENT INTEREST WHATSOEVER IN: REAL ESTATE

MINIMUM AND MAXIMUM INVESTMENT DOLLAR AMOUNT: VARIES

HOWARD LAWSON & CO

GENESIS FUND

2 Penn Center Plaza

Philadelphia, PA 19102-1701

PHONE #: 215-988-0010

FAX #: 215-568-0029

AREA OF INVESTMENT REGION CONSIDERED: EASTERN UNITED STATES

MOST DESIRED INVESTMENTS IN FIELDS OF: HIGH TECHNOLOGY, MANUFACTURING COMPANIES, ELECTRONICS

POSSIBLE CONSIDERATION FOR INVESTMENT IN: NO OTHER FIELDS

NO INVESTMENT INTEREST WHATSOEVER IN: ALL OTHER FIELDS. NO START-UP COMPANIES

MINIMUM AND MAXIMUM INVESTMENT DOLLAR AMOUNT: $500,000 to $1,500,000

PROVIDENCE VENTURES INC

50 Kennedy Plaza.

9th Floor

Providence, RI 02903

PHONE #: 401-751-1700

FAX #: 401-751-9340

AREA OF INVESTMENT REGION CONSIDERED: UNITED STATES

MOST DESIRED INVESTMENTS IN FIELDS OF: CABLE, T.V., MEDIA COMMUNICATIONS

POSSIBLE CONSIDERATION FOR INVESTMENT IN: NO OTHER FIELDS

NO INVESTMENT INTEREST WHATSOEVER IN: ALL OTHER FIELDS

MINIMUM AND MAXIMUM INVESTMENT DOLLAR AMOUNT: VARIES

FLEET EQUITY PARTNERS

111 Westminster St.

Providence, RI 02903

PHONE #: 401-278-6770

FAX #: 401-278-6387

AREA OF INVESTMENT REGION CONSIDERED: UNITED STATES

MOST DESIRED INVESTMENTS IN FIELDS OF: PRINTING COMPANIES, PUBLISHING, MEDICAL HEALTH CARE PRODUCTS, MEDICAL HEALTH CARE SERVICES, LOW TECHNOLOGY COMPANIES

POSSIBLE CONSIDERATION FOR INVESTMENT IN: OPEN TO OTHER INVEST-MENTS IN SIMILAR FIELDS

NO INVESTMENT INTEREST WHATSOEVER IN: NO START-UP COMPANIES, COMPUTERS, FINANCIAL SERVICES , HIGH TECHNOLOGY OR BIOTECHNOLOGY COMPANIES OR ANY OTHER FIELDS

MINIMUM AND MAXIMUM INVESTMENT DOLLAR AMOUNT: $5,000,000+

PALMETTO SEED CAPITAL CORP.

P. O. Box 17526

Greensville, SC 29606

PHONE #: 803-232-6198

FAX #: 803-271-8374

AREA OF INVESTMENT REGION CONSIDERED: SOUTH CAROLINA ONLY

MOST DESIRED INVESTMENTS IN FIELDS OF: OPEN TO MANY INVESTMENTS. HIGH TECHNOLOGY, COMPUTER PRODUCTS, BIOTECHNOLOGY, INFORMATIONAL SERVICES, SERVICE COMPANIES, ELECTRONICS, LIFE SCIENCES, ENVIRONMENTAL, MANUFACTURING, COMMUNICATIONS

POSSIBLE CONSIDERATION FOR INVESTMENT IN: START-UP COMPANIES, OPEN TO OTHER PROPOSALS

NO INVESTMENT INTEREST WHATSOEVER IN: REAL ESTATE, OIL OR GAS

MINIMUM AND MAXIMUM INVESTMENT DOLLAR AMOUNT: VARIES

FRANKLIN VENTURE CAPITAL INC

237 2nd Ave. S.
Franklin, TN 37064
PHONE #: 615-791-9462
FAX #: 615-791-9636

AREA OF INVESTMENT REGION CONSIDERED: UNITED STATES

MOST DESIRED INVESTMENTS IN FIELDS OF: MEDICAL HEALTH CARE PRODUCTS, MEDICAL HEALTH CARE SERVICE COMPANIES, CONSUMER PRODUCTS

POSSIBLE CONSIDERATION FOR INVESTMENT IN: NO OTHER FIELDS

NO INVESTMENT INTEREST WHATSOEVER IN: ALL OTHER FIELDS

MINIMUM AND MAXIMUM INVESTMENT DOLLAR AMOUNT: $500,000 to $1,500,000

TENNESSEE VENTURE CAPITAL CORP

1451 Elmhill Pike, #316

Nashville, TN 37210

PHONE #: 615-366-2050

FAX #: 615-367-0464

AREA OF INVESTMENT REGION CONSIDERED: TENNESSEE ONLY

MOST DESIRED INVESTMENTS IN FIELDS OF: OPEN TO MANY INVESTMENTS FOR MINORITIES

POSSIBLE CONSIDERATION FOR INVESTMENT IN: SOME START-UP COMPANIES

NO INVESTMENT INTEREST WHATSOEVER IN: REAL ESTATE

MINIMUM AND MAXIMUM INVESTMENT DOLLAR AMOUNT: VARIES

MASSEY BURCH INVESTMENT GROUP INC

310 25th Ave N.

Suite 103

Nashville, TN 37203-1515

PHONE #: 615-329-9448

FAX #: 615-329-9237

AREA OF INVESTMENT REGION CONSIDERED: SOUTHERN U.S.

MOST DESIRED INVESTMENTS IN FIELDS OF: HIGH TECHNOLOGY, MEDICAL HEALTH CARE COMPANIES, ELECTRONICS, LIFE SCIENCES, MEDICAL HEALTH CARE SERVICES

POSSIBLE CONSIDERATION FOR INVESTMENT IN: SOME START-UP COMPANIES

NO INVESTMENT INTEREST WHATSOEVER IN: ALL OTHER FIELDS

MINIMUM AND MAXIMUM INVESTMENT DOLLAR AMOUNT: $500,000+

DAVIS VENTURE PARTNERS

2121 San Jacinto St.

Suite 975

Dallas, TX 75201

PHONE #: 214-954-1822

FAX #: 214-969-0256

AREA OF INVESTMENT REGION CONSIDERED: SOUTH WEST & SOUTH CENTRAL US.

MOST DESIRED INVESTMENTS IN FIELDS OF: OPEN TO MANY INVESTMENTS. HIGH TECHNOLOGY, COMPUTER PRODUCTS, BIOTECHNOLOGY, INFORMATIONAL SERVICES, ELECTRONICS, LIFE SCIENCES, ENVIRONMENTAL, SERVICE COMPANIES, MANUFACTURING, COMMUNICATIONS

POSSIBLE CONSIDERATION FOR INVESTMENT IN: SOME START-UP COMPANIES, OPEN TO OTHER PROPOSALS

NO INVESTMENT INTEREST WHATSOEVER IN: REAL ESTATE, OIL OR GAS

MINIMUM AND MAXIMUM INVESTMENT DOLLAR AMOUNT: $1,000,000 to $10,000,000+

CAPITAL SOUTHWEST MANAGEMENT

12900 Preston Rd.

Suite 700

Dallas, TX 75230

PHONE #: 214-233-8242

FAX #: 214-233-7362

AREA OF INVESTMENT REGION CONSIDERED: UNITED STATES

MOST DESIRED INVESTMENTS IN FIELDS OF: MANUFACTURING, LOW TECHNOLOGY, SPECIAL RETAIL, DISTRIBUTION WHOLESALER

POSSIBLE CONSIDERATION FOR INVESTMENT IN: NO OTHER FIELDS

NO INVESTMENT INTEREST WHATSOEVER IN: START-UP COMPANIES AND ALL OTHER FIELDS

MINIMUM AND MAXIMUM INVESTMENT DOLLAR AMOUNT: $1,000,000 to $3,000,000

MESBIC VENTURES HOLDINGS CO.

12655 N. Central Expressway

Suite 710

Dallas, TX 75243

PHONE #: 214-991-1597

FAX #: 214-991-1647

AREA OF INVESTMENT REGION CONSIDERED: UNITED STATES, MAJORITY OF INVESTMENTS IN TEXAS

MOST DESIRED INVESTMENTS IN FIELDS OF: OPEN TO MANY FIELDS. COMPUTER HARDWARE, SOFTWARE, HIGH TECHNOLOGY, MANUFACTURING, COMMUNICATIONS

POSSIBLE CONSIDERATION FOR INVESTMENT IN: MAY CONSIDER EARLY STAGE COMPANIES

NO INVESTMENT INTEREST WHATSOEVER IN: REAL ESTATE OIL OR GAS OR START-UP COMPANIES

MINIMUM AND MAXIMUM INVESTMENT DOLLAR AMOUNT: $300,000+

TRIAD VENTURES LTD

4600 Post Oak Place

Suite 2530

Houston, TX 77027

PHONE #: 713-627-9111

FAX #: 713-627-9119

AREA OF INVESTMENT REGION CONSIDERED: TEXAS

MOST DESIRED INVESTMENTS IN FIELDS OF: HIGH TECHNOLOGY, MANUFACTURING

POSSIBLE CONSIDERATION FOR INVESTMENT IN: ESTABLISHED COMPANIES IN THESE FIELDS ONLY

NO INVESTMENT INTEREST WHATSOEVER IN: START-UP COMPANIES

MINIMUM AND MAXIMUM INVESTMENT DOLLAR AMOUNT: $500,000+

DAVIS VENTURE PARTNERS

515 Post Oak Blvd.

Suite 250

Houston, TX 77027

PHONE #: 713-993-0440

FAX #: 713-621-2297

AREA OF INVESTMENT REGION CONSIDERED: SOUTH WEST & SOUTH CENTRAL US.

MOST DESIRED INVESTMENTS IN FIELDS OF: OPEN TO MANY INVESTMENTS. HIGH TECHNOLOGY, COMPUTER PRODUCTS, BIOTECHNOLOGY, INFORMATIONAL SERVICES, ELECTRONICS, LIFE SCIENCES, ENVIRONMENTAL, SERVICE COMPANIES, MANUFACTURING, COMMUNICATIONS

POSSIBLE CONSIDERATION FOR INVESTMENT IN: SOME START-UP COMPANIES, OPEN TO OTHER PROPOSALS

NO INVESTMENT INTEREST WHATSOEVER IN: REAL ESTATE, OIL OR GAS

MINIMUM AND MAXIMUM INVESTMENT DOLLAR AMOUNT: $1,000,000 to $10,000,000+

SOUTHWEST VENTURE PARTNERS

16414 San Pedro, #345

San Antonio, TX 78232

PHONE #: 210-402-1200

FAX #: 210-402-1221

AREA OF INVESTMENT REGION CONSIDERED: UNITED STATES

MOST DESIRED INVESTMENTS IN FIELDS OF: BIOTECHNOLOGY, MEDICAL HEALTH CARE PRODUCTS, HIGH TECHNOLOGY, ENVIRONMENTAL, ELECTRONICS, LIFE SCIENCES, MEDICAL HEALTH CARE SERVICES

POSSIBLE CONSIDERATION FOR INVESTMENT IN: NO OTHER FIELDS

NO INVESTMENT INTEREST WHATSOEVER IN: ALL OTHER FIELDS

MINIMUM AND MAXIMUM INVESTMENT DOLLAR AMOUNT: $1,000,000+

AUSTIN VENTURES

1300 Norwood Tower

114 W. 7th St.

Austin, TX 78701

PHONE #: 512-479-0055

FAX #: 512-476-3942

AREA OF INVESTMENT REGION CONSIDERED: TEXAS AND SOUTHWEST

MOST DESIRED INVESTMENTS IN FIELDS OF: TELECOMMUNICATIONS, CABLE, SPECIALITY RETAIL, MANUFACTURING, MULTI-MEDIA

POSSIBLE CONSIDERATION FOR INVESTMENT IN: NO OTHER FIELDS

NO INVESTMENT INTEREST WHATSOEVER IN: ALL OTHER FIELDS

MINIMUM AND MAXIMUM INVESTMENT DOLLAR AMOUNT: $2,000,000+

APPLIED TECHNOLOGY

2111 Highgrove Terrace

Austin, TX 78703

PHONE #: 512-479-8622

FAX #: 512-474-5126

AREA OF INVESTMENT REGION CONSIDERED: UNITED STATES

MOST DESIRED INVESTMENTS IN FIELDS OF: START-UP COMPANIES, DATA COMMUNICATIONS, ELECTRONICS, ENVIRONMENTAL, DATA PROCESSING, INFORMATION SERVICES, HIGH TECHNOLOGY COMMUNICATIONS, MULTIMEDIA, CD ROM

POSSIBLE CONSIDERATION FOR INVESTMENT IN: NO OTHER FIELDS

NO INVESTMENT INTEREST WHATSOEVER IN: ALL OTHER FIELDS

MINIMUM AND MAXIMUM INVESTMENT DOLLAR AMOUNT: $100,000 to $1,000,000

CURETON & CO., INC.

1200 Travis

Suite 2050

Houston, TX 77002-6062

PHONE #: 713-658-9806

FAX #: 713-658-0476

AREA OF INVESTMENT REGION CONSIDERED: TEXAS, OKLAHOMA, LOUISIANA, ARKANSAS

MOST DESIRED INVESTMENTS IN FIELDS OF: OPEN TO MANY INVESTMENTS. HIGH TECHNOLOGY, COMPUTER PRODUCTS, BIOTECHNOLOGY, ELECTRONICS, LIFE SCIENCES, ENVIRONMENTAL, INFORMATIONAL SERVICES, MANUFACTURING, COMMUNICATIONS

POSSIBLE CONSIDERATION FOR INVESTMENT IN: SOME START-UP COMPANIES, OPEN TO OTHER PROPOSALS

NO INVESTMENT INTEREST WHATSOEVER IN: REAL ESTATE, OIL OR GAS

MINIMUM AND MAXIMUM INVESTMENT DOLLAR AMOUNT: $1,000,000+

OLYMPIC VENTURE PARTNERS

2420 Carillon Point

Kirkland, WA 98033

PHONE #: 206-889-9192

AREA OF INVESTMENT REGION CONSIDERED: WESTERN U.S.

MOST DESIRED INVESTMENTS IN FIELDS OF: HIGH TECHNOLOGY, MEDICAL HEALTH CARE PRODUCTS, MEDICAL HEALTH CARE SERVICES

POSSIBLE CONSIDERATION FOR INVESTMENT IN: PREFERS START-UP COMPANIES IN THESE FIELDS ONLY

NO INVESTMENT INTEREST WHATSOEVER IN: ALL OTHER FIELDS

MINIMUM AND MAXIMUM INVESTMENT DOLLAR AMOUNT: $100,000 to $1,500,000

CABLE & HOWSE VENTURES

777 108th Ave., N.E.

Suite 2300

Bellevue, WA 98004-5118

PHONE #: 206-646-3030

FAX #: 206-646-3041

AREA OF INVESTMENT REGION CONSIDERED: UNITED STATES

MOST DESIRED INVESTMENTS IN FIELDS OF: HIGH TECHNOLOGY, BIOTECHNOLOGY, INFORMATIONAL SERVICES, ELECTRONICS, LIFE SCIENCES, ENVIRONMENTAL, COMPUTER SOFTWARE, COMMUNICATIONS

POSSIBLE CONSIDERATION FOR INVESTMENT IN: SOME START-UP COMPANIES

NO INVESTMENT INTEREST WHATSOEVER IN: ALL OTHER FIELDS

MINIMUM AND MAXIMUM INVESTMENT DOLLAR AMOUNT: $100,000 to $1,000,000

M & I VENTURES CORP

770 N. Water St.

11th Floor

Milwaukee, WI 53202

PHONE #: 414-765-7910

FAX #: 414-765-7850

AREA OF INVESTMENT REGION CONSIDERED: MIDWEST UNITED STATES

MOST DESIRED INVESTMENTS IN FIELDS OF: OPEN TO MANY INVESTMENTS. HIGH TECHNOLOGY, COMPUTER PRODUCTS, BIOTECHNOLOGY, INFORMATIONAL SERVICES, ELECTRONICS, LIFE SCIENCES, ENVIRONMENTAL, SERVICE COMPANIES, MANUFACTURING, COMMUNICATIONS

POSSIBLE CONSIDERATION FOR INVESTMENT IN: OPEN TO OTHER PROPOSALS

NO INVESTMENT INTEREST WHATSOEVER IN: START-UP COMPANIES, REAL ESTATE, OIL OR GAS

MINIMUM AND MAXIMUM INVESTMENT DOLLAR AMOUNT: $1,000,000+

VENTURES INVESTORS WISCONSIN INC

924 E. Juneau Ave.

Suite 617

Milwaukee, WI 53202

PHONE #: 414-272-4400

FAX #: 414-272-4327

AREA OF INVESTMENT REGION CONSIDERED: WISCONSIN

MOST DESIRED INVESTMENTS IN FIELDS OF: HIGH TECHNOLOGY, LEADING EDGE TECHNOLOGY ONLY

POSSIBLE CONSIDERATION FOR INVESTMENT IN: SOME START-UP COMPANIES IN THESE FIELDS ONLY

NO INVESTMENT INTEREST WHATSOEVER IN: ALL OTHER COMPANIES

MINIMUM AND MAXIMUM INVESTMENT DOLLAR AMOUNT: VARIES

HORIZON PARTNERS, LTD.

225 E. Mason St.

Suite 600

Milwaukee, WI 53202

PHONE #: 414-271-2200

FAX #: 414-271-4016

AREA OF INVESTMENT REGION CONSIDERED: UNITED STATES

MOST DESIRED INVESTMENTS IN FIELDS OF: OPEN TO MANY INVESTMENTS. HIGH TECHNOLOGY, COMPUTER PRODUCTS, BIOTECHNOLOGY, INFORMATIONAL SERVICES, ELECTRONICS, LIFE SCIENCES, ENVIRONMENTAL, SERVICE COMPANIES, MANUFACTURING, COMMUNICATIONS

POSSIBLE CONSIDERATION FOR INVESTMENT IN: OPEN TO OTHER PROPOSALS

NO INVESTMENT INTEREST WHATSOEVER IN: REAL ESTATE, OIL OR GAS

MINIMUM AND MAXIMUM INVESTMENT DOLLAR AMOUNT: $500,000+

LUBAR & CO.

777 E. Wisconsin Ave.

Suite 3380

Milwaukee, WI 53202

PHONE #: 414-291-9000

FAX #: 414-291-9061

AREA OF INVESTMENT REGION CONSIDERED: UNITED STATES

MOST DESIRED INVESTMENTS IN FIELDS OF: OPEN TO MANY INVESTMENTS. HIGH TECHNOLOGY, COMPUTER PRODUCTS, BIOTECHNOLOGY, INFORMATIONAL SERVICES, ELECTRONICS, LIFE SCIENCES, ENVIRONMENTAL, SERVICE COMPANIES, MANUFACTURING, COMMUNICATIONS

POSSIBLE CONSIDERATION FOR INVESTMENT IN: SOME START-UP COMPANIES, OPEN TO OTHER PROPOSALS

NO INVESTMENT INTEREST WHATSOEVER IN: REAL ESTATE, OIL OR GAS

MINIMUM AND MAXIMUM INVESTMENT DOLLAR AMOUNT: $1,000,000+

MATRIX VENTURE FUNDS INC

13255 W. Bluemound Rd.

Brookfield, WI 53005-6245

PHONE #: 414-789-0202

FAX #: 414-789-0204

AREA OF INVESTMENT REGION CONSIDERED: WISCONSIN

MOST DESIRED INVESTMENTS IN FIELDS OF: SMALL MANUFACTURING COMPANIES ONLY

POSSIBLE CONSIDERATION FOR INVESTMENT IN: SMALL DEALS ONLY

NO INVESTMENT INTEREST WHATSOEVER IN: NO HIGH TECHNOLOGY OR BIOTECHNOLOGY

MINIMUM AND MAXIMUM INVESTMENT DOLLAR AMOUNT: $250,000+

About the Author

Philip C. Paul's career in sales, marketing, and finance spans three decades. As a member of the Mortgage Bankers Association and Mortgage Brokers Association, he has financed over $250 million dollars in loans. The author owned and operated three mortgage companies for the past seven years and raised millions of dollars in capital for many other corporations. This was accomplished through the use of venture capitalists and private placements. He also raised capital for other corporations by taking companies public into the stock market. Paul's knowledge in the fields of finance, manufacturing, and marketing, enabled him to pen the reference book dealing with manufacturers' sales representatives titled, ***Let the Pros Sell It.***

During his investment years, Paul discovered that many entrepreneurs did not know how to obtain capital to start a new company or to continue the growth of their existing companies. This fact became very apparent when he owned the mortgage companies, and was overwhelmed with loan requests for capital. With the current banking system and banking policies, venture capital was hard to obtain. Over the years, he has compiled an extensive list of venture capital firms — firms that have billions of dollars ready to loan or invest in companies — and made this list available for use and profit. ***Where To Find Venture Capital, A Resource Guide,*** is now available to the public.

All entrepreneurs must know how and where to find venture capital when needed and ***Where To Find Venture Capital, A Resource Guide*** can make the difference between success and failure.